To: Brian!

D1196371

# GERONIMO

## 8 JUMPS TO YOUR
## SUPERCALIFRAGILISTICEXPIALIDOCIOUS LIFE

*Keep Jumping*

*&*

*Keep the Faith*

## MARK E. BATTIATO
Co-Founder, Growth Into Greatness Institute

Mr. Brian, Yes I recently published this ...
it's not really a Business Book but Life
Book ... Applies to All area's of Life ... Hope it
inspires you to keep Jumping in 2021!
MERRY CHRISTMAS 2020

Inquiries regarding permission for use of the material contained in this book should be addressed to:

**Growth Into Greatness Institute**
mark@greatnessinstitute.com
greatnessinstitute.com

ISBN-13: 978-1-7334942-0-5

CREDITS:

*Copy Editor:* Debbie Barrett, Word Paper Scissors

*Design:* Kendra Cagle, 5 Lakes Design

*Marketing:* Leon Smith Publishing

# TABLE OF CONTENTS

# ACKNOWLEDGEMENTS

*"The fool doth think he is wise, but the wise person
knows themselves to be a fool."*

– SHAKESPEARE

In creating this book, I know the above to be true. I want to thank all the people who believed in me who are too many to mention, but most importantly my mother and father, Lucien and Donna Battiato; my brother, Vic, and my sister, Pat all my family in Chicago; my mother-in-law, JoAnn Capps; my beautiful wife, Christy; my two amazing children, Brandon and Sophia; the late Bill Bailey; Jim Rohn; the many doctors I am privileged to work with, especially Dr. Michael Schuster; my father-in-law who reignited my passion for personal growth and development and my business partners at Growth into Greatness Institute, Deb Castillo, and Dr. Kevin Kwiecien, who are more friends than colleagues. I would also like to acknowledge my clients and people who have become life-long cherished friends: Blair Kolkoski, Dr. Karen O'Donnell, Dr. Paul Falvey, Dr. Peter Fay, Dr. Bob Gottlieb, Dr. Doug Sandquist, Dr. Andy Cohen, Brian DesRoches, Dr. Tim Leary, Jim Logan, Greg Zlevor, Kirk Behrendt, Jeremy Allen, Jonathan Johnston, Kurt Clink, Marc Salvatore, Jim Breeze, Larry Hodge, Patrick Larsen, Dr. John Kois, Bruce Sherbourne, and so many others unnamed. Thank you. I am truly grateful to all of you for enriching my life. Lastly, to my source of life, my true Friend and Everlasting Father, Creator, Jesus, who still believes in my foolish ways. If the words in this book can help anyone take just one Geronimo Jump, it is all worthwhile.

*"I will lift my eyes to the hills, from where cometh my help. My help
cometh from the Lord, which made Heaven and Earth"*

– PSALM 121

i

# FOREWORD

How did the title "Geronimo" come to be? I grew up in Chicago and went to college in Arizona where I fell in love with the West, the mountains and the ocean.

When our children were 5- and 3-years-old, we moved to Oregon where we lived for 17 years. When we decided to move back to the desert in Arizona, it was a Geronimo jump. This move was a significant jump because I knew it would force me out of my comfort zone, and I was pretty content without much challenge in my life. First, we were settled in our small community. I loved my boat, which I would have to sell because I couldn't to bring it to Arizona. And I had always enjoyed driving to the Oregon Coast; the beach and the scenery were spectacular, and I loved the ocean and the mountains. Further, I had a great group of men friends who I was in the habit of meeting every Wednesday and Friday morning. Add to that, I was just two years shy of paying off the mortgage on our Oregon home, so the risk of buying another home, which was double the cost of our home in Oregon, was a big jump! I was 55-years-old. Making house payments for another 15 to 30 years didn't seem too smart. My mentor at the time asked me if my wife, Christy, wanted to move to Arizona and leave our Medford community after 17 years. When I explained to him that her family was there, and that she had actually wanted to move back to Arizona for the past five years, he said, "Marcus, I suggest you move back without delay." I countered, "But I love this area and my house is almost paid off." Then he said, "Marcus, this is not about you! It will be a great move for you. So just do it!"

As it turned out, leaving behind relationships and a neighborhood that we'd known was just the jump I needed to bring us all to a new chapter in our lives, a new beginning and adventure.

My daughter, who was 18-years-old at the time, found a home online that she thought we would be happy in because the house was modern, and had a small swimming pool. It was surrounded by mountains, and it was only five minutes from my daughter's two cousins, who she enjoyed spending time with. The home just so happened to be located on a street called, you guessed it, "Geronimo." I was not going to even look at the home because the photos did not look that great, and the price was a little high for me. But as fate would have it, when we went out to Arizona to look for houses, this was the second home we looked at, and we took the jump. We now live on that street called "Geronimo." I looked up the word "Geronimo" for fun and found the meanings very intriguing. I've been wanting to write a book for the last ten years about taking the right kind of chances to live a fulfilling life, and Geronimo was the perfect title. What you hold in your hands is the outcome of trials, experiences, wisdom, mentors and friends who helped form the 8 Geronimo jumps.

Now, why the word "Supercalifragilisticexpialidocious?" I just thought it sounded fun! I did look up the word as well and the definition of Su-per-ca-li-fra-gil-is-tic-ex-pi-a-li-do-cious is "extraordinarily good; wonderful." I like that. Wonderful, good. Wonder being the root word of wonderful. I wonder what jumps could help us all move towards Wonderful, good? This would be a worthy goal in life.

During the time of the writing of this book, my father, Lucien Battiato passed on to his new wonderful life. I was blessed to have a wonderful, good father of 84 years. I know many young boys, men and daughters did not or cannot say this. My father was a wonderful man. I often share with people that I never heard my "Italian" father yell or scream growing up. I found out later why this was. When I was around 30-years-old, I went out to lunch with him in downtown Chicago. At the restaurant, we met a priest who had befriended my dad. My dad told the priest and I that when he was 20, he made commitment to not become like his father, my grandfather who yelled at my dad a lot as he was growing up. As I look back, I see that my father honored that commitment. In fact, I never heard my father say a negative comment about another human being, especially about my mother, brother or sister or me. My father lived a super- califragisticexpialodocious life!

No, it was not perfect. He made mistakes. I'm sure he experienced negative thoughts and anger, but he made the internal Geronimo Jump to live a different life, a better way. As Og Mandino, a very popular author who has written over 20 books on personal growth, would say, "We're all searching for a better way to live, I believe. Who would not want to find a better way to live, love, be in this one life we're given."

My hope is this book gives you some insights from my short 58 years on this earth to navigate the jumps that will move you from success to significance. Thanks, Dad, for making a meaningful impact in my life and helping me take many jumps that I would have not attempted alone. We all need each other in life. Lisa Nichols, a celebrated motivational speaker who has inspired millions through her role as a featured teacher in The Secant, once said, "You gotta jump to be the best version of you."

The eight Geronimo jumps are in no particular order and you could start with any one of them. For me, they are all significant jumps I needed to make, and I'm still jumping deeper in to each one.

Once you begin jumping just like my daughter, Sophia at age 4 on our backyard trampoline you can always jump a little higher. On a trampoline, it's never the first jump that launches you the highest. You have to keep jumping to get the momentum going to reach your highest point. Enjoy the Geronimo 8 Jumps and make your life supercalifragilisticexpialidocious!

# PERIOD OF DESTINY TIME CHART

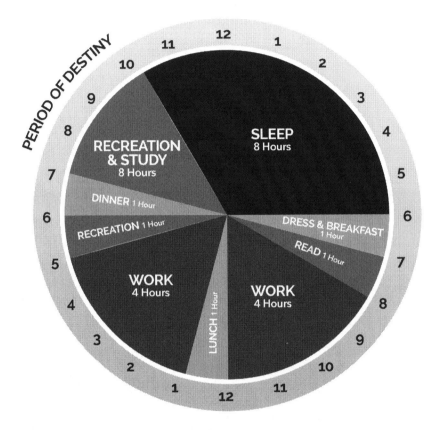

| | |
|---|---|
| Sleep | 8 hours |
| Dress and Breakfast | 1 hour |
| Work | 4 hours |
| Lunch | 1 hour |
| Work | 4 hours |
| Dinner | 1 hour |
| Recreation and Study | 5 hours |
| **TOTAL** | **24 HOURS** |

Someone once gave me the Period of Destiny diagram (above). This model gives us the opportunity to jump into a life of meaning and purpose each day; if followed, it gives us the chance to make a difference for ourselves and others. The Period of Destiny model contains a good daily reminder that we all have a choice to challenge ourselves to live that life, or destiny, we want to live. Whether that Period of Destiny is 30 minutes or three hours, the point is to spend that quality time in pursuit of something significant. Whether you are reading, jumping on a trampoline, learning a new skill, or taking a new hike, or volunteering, it's about evolving and examining your heart, mind, and soul. Simply by reading this book, you're working on your Period of Destiny. Commit to pursuing significant leaps to fly higher, to soaring like eagles. Even though in this life we may never actually fly without help, we can still jump into a better way to live, in the pursuit of our destiny.

You might remember in the movie, "The Last Samurai," played by Tom Cruise, when they are about to prepare for battle and the leader of the Samurai warriors asked the commander, "You believe a man can change his destiny? He answers, "I think a man does what he can, until his destiny is revealed."

My friend and business partner at the Growth into Greatness Institute, Deb Castillo, always says, "It will be revealed, Mark." May the insights in this book do just that: move you closer towards your destiny and the life you could only imagine!

# GERONIMO JUMP 1

---

# TRUMPETS
# CALL JUMP

*"You've gotta JUMP to be the best version of you."*
—LISA NICHOLS

In the movie, "The First Knight," starring Richard Gere and Sean Connery (1995), Gere is trying to win the heart of Guinevere, played by Julia Ormond. But first, Gere, as Sir Lancelot, must jump onto a platform called the Gauntlet and run through a series of jumps, sharp pendulums, swords, spikes, death traps and more to reach his ultimate destiny. . . Guinevere, the love of his life. Before Lancelot jumps onto the Gauntlet, the trumpets sound in the background. Trumpets call us higher to seize the day, to jump to reach higher, to see glory within and jump into the greatness awaiting us – our destiny.

I was never told about the trumpets call until one fateful day in Chicago at a 2-day professional development event led by Jim Rohn, a leading author and business philosopher who taught around the world for over three decades. Rohn was my mentor on personal growth and development. I had heard the name William E Bailey mentioned once by Rohn who said that Mr. Bailey was *his* greatest mentor, and that he was in the room that day. At one point, Jim asked William to stand, and 500 plus people passionately applauded, as I did, for a person we had never heard of. My brother-in-law, Blair Kolkoski, who was with me, said, "we have got to meet his guy." But at each break, Bailey was mobbed by people.

The second day, with only two hours left of the seminar, there was a break and I needed to use the restroom. As fate would have it, William E. Bailey was taking a break at the same time. I said, "Hello. You're Bill Bailey!" "Yes, I am," he said, "nice to meet you." We did not shake hands, for obvious reasons, but he suggested we meet. Outside the men's room, we struck up a conversation, and the next thing I knew, he said, "Mark, I would like to visit you in Arizona. I love to play golf so let's make that happen." I just thought, this will never happen; Bill would not travel all the way from Kentucky where he lived, to Arizona, just to play golf with me. We exchanged phone numbers and, lo and behold, Bill called me the following week and asked when could he come visit. I was so surprised, and of course I said yes, and invited him to stay at our home. When I told Christy, she asked, "Who is this man?" I said, "Jim Rohn said he was his mentor." That's all the introduction he needed.

I share this story because for the next 10 to 15 years, Bill called me once a week. He made many trips to Arizona, and I visited him in Kentucky. One of the most incredible times was when I went with Bill to Jim Rohn's house, where we spent two days together. Before Bill and Jim, I had never really had mentors. Not only were they older and wiser, their key philosophy was about personal and continuous growth, a very pertinent message for me. Bill took me under his wing, and for four years, we lectured together and ran retreats entitled "Secrets from the Mountains," which featured spiritual lessons for a successful life. Both Bill and Jim would share their wisdom, and we all encouraged each other's' walks in life. And we helped each other jump.

To this day, I believe my meeting up with Bill was no accident. Sometimes people literally jump into your life, and Bill was that for me. It was truly a trumpet's call.

The poem below was written by Bill. For over 30 years, he carried the lines around in his head. He appropriately called it "The Warrior's Song." He shared it with me over the phone with complete memory of when it first came to him while he was in the mountains one early morning while camping alone. He said he does not question the source of where it came.

Here are the words that impacted my life and the lives of so many others:

## WARRIOR'S SONG
POEM BY WILLIAM E. BAILEY FROM HIS BOOK, RHYTHMS OF LIFE

*The sun kisses a mountain top*
*And glistens on its face of snow,*
*And slowly climbs into the sky above*
*And lights the valley below.*

*For each of us that this day awakes*
*A miracle takes place.*
*For once again we walk our earth*
*And own all upon its face.*

*And the past regrets and foolish fears*
*Of yesterday's cloudy mind,*
*Are washed away by the light of day*
*And seem so far behind.*

*For each of us is reborn each day, Our life renews again.*
*And with the help of God we will find a cause*
*That makes us want to win.*

*For a person without a goal in life*
*Is a person already dead.*
*Their mind wanders from place to place,*
*And he walks with feet of lead.*

*They have no reason to stretch their mind, No spirit to stir their soul.*
*Their name is not even in the book, When destiny calls the roll.*

*Better to take the wine of life*
*And drink both deep and long –*
*Greet each day 'cause you're here to stay,*
*And sing your warrior's song.*

*For the battle of life is joined, and*
*You must fight long and true*
*For in this strife, it's the game of your life*
*And the only loser is you.*


*Gird up your loins with courage*
*And answer the trumpets call,*
*And lose or win, you can say at the end,*
*This was the greatest of all!*

– WILLIAM E. BAILEY

The last stanza of the poem, I've never forgotten: "gird up your loins with courage," for in life we will face many difficulties, challenges, and obstacles, and if we quiet ourselves and listen, the trumpet will call us back to the fray. Scott Peck, who wrote the famous book "The Road Less Traveled," said this: "Life is difficult. This is a great truth, one of the greatest truths. It is a great truth because, once we truly see this truth, we transcend it. Once we truly know that life is difficult, once we truly understand and accept it – then life is no longer difficult. Because, once it is accepted, the fact that life is difficult no longer matters."

As Bill Bailey says, "for each of us is reborn each day, our life renews again, and with the help of God, we will find a cause that makes us want to win."

Each day is a new day to jump. Maybe it's just clearing a little hedge – maybe it's just jumping out of bed when it's tempting to roll over and hit the snooze button. Someone once told me to forget saying alarm clock and say "opportunity clock!" New day!

Many of you have heard of the poem by Robert Frost called "The Road Not Taken." Read his words. They are just as powerful as Bill Bailey's "The Warrior's Song."

## THE ROAD NOT TAKEN

*Two roads diverged in a yellow wood,*
*And sorry I could not travel both,*
*And be one traveler, long I stood*
*And looked down one as far as I could,*
*To where it bent in the undergrowth . . ."*

Robert Frost reminds us that there are two roads, two mountains, two choices – and we must choose . . . we must jump; we must listen to the trumpet's call and leap, or destiny will not be revealed to us. As the Warrior's Song says, "better to take the wine of life and drink both deep and long - greet each day 'cause you're here to stay and sing your warrior's song."

*"For the battle of life is joined, and*
*You must fight long and true..*
*For in this strife, it's the game of your life*
*And the only loser is you."*

Tough words, but true nonetheless. As Shakespeare once said, "The truth is incontrovertible. Malice may attack it, ignorance may deride it, but in the end, there it is."

The Trumpet's Call Jump is a call to action, a sound to leap, to continue to jump in all areas of our life. In the movie, "The Book of Eli," the apocalypse has occurred, and there is one last remaining book of the Bible. "Eli," played by Denzel Washington, hears the trumpets call to carry it across thousands of miles to deliver it for a new beginning. Eli must jump through many obstacles to deliver the book, and he eventually encounters death. But his last words are "I have fought the good fight, I have finished the race, I have kept the faith."

Don't all of us desire this for our soul? To finish strong? To fight the good fight? If you take the Geronimo Jumps, you will indeed experience new depth, new insights, new revelations of what your purpose is in this one life you have been given.

Speaking of revelation, allow me to share something you might possibly have never heard or read on the Trumpet's Call. In the book of Numbers in the Bible, not a very popular book, nonetheless, it speaks on the Trumpet's Call.

*"And the Lord spake unto Moses saying, Make thee two trumpets of silver; of a whole piece shalt thee make them."*
—NUMBERS 10:1, 2

In the days before megaphones, telephones, or cell phones, one of the ways to communicate would be through the sounding of the trumpets. Two trumpets were to be made of silver to be sounded for four specific reasons.

The first reason the trumpets sounded was for convocation - when the people were to assemble at the door of the tabernacle. The second reason the trumpets were sounded was for the purpose of mobilization - to tell the people it was time to pull up stakes, pack up their tents, and move ahead. Said another way - Geronimo jump! The third reason was for confrontation – to do battle against the enemies which the children of Israel would encounter in the Promised Land. The fourth and final reason the trumpets were to sound was the purpose of celebration – to signal the feast and festivals as well as the solemn days.

Everything in the Old Testament is an illustration of New Testament truth – and the trumpets made of silver, the metal of redemption, are no exception, for they give us understanding about which Paul the Apostle called a mystery . . .

> *"Behold; I shew you a mystery; we shall not all sleep,*
> *but we shall be changed in the twinkling of an eye,*
> *at the last trump: for the trumpets shall sound, and the*
> *dead shall be raised incorruptible, and we shall be changed."*
> —1 CORINTHIANS 15:51, 52

We will speak more about the Trumpet call in chapter 8, exploring more about what that Geronimo call will mean for your transformation, your living a supercalifragilisticexpialidocious life!

Before we move into the 2nd jump, let's take a look at some Trumpet's calls to action through the lens of David Lee Roth, an early 80's rocker and member of the original Van Halen group.

## JUMP

*Owwww!*

*I get up, and nothin' gets me down*

*You got it tough, I've seen the toughest around*

*And I know, baby, just how you feel*

*You got to roll with the punches and get to what's real*

*Ah, can't ya see me standin' here*

*I got my back against the record machine*

*I ain't the worst that you've seen*

*Ah, can't ya see what I mean?*

*Ah, might as well jump. Jump!*

— LYRICS BY VAN HALEN

# TRUMPETS CALL JUMP

## JUMPING CALLS TO ACTION

- Each morning or evening, meditate, journal or think quietly; reflect on your life.

- Carve out your Period of Destiny (see chart on next page) so you might begin to hear the trumpet's call, even if it's just 15 minutes.

- Reflect on The Warrior's Song. Write your most important goals on 3x5 index cards. Carry them with you, review, reflect.

- Search out guides, mentors, people you admire in life. These could be people in your own back yard. Consider family, a close friend at work, someone you meet at a seminar who spoke and they seem to muster the Trumpet's call in you.

# GERONIMO JUMP 2

---

# FREEDOM JUMP

*"On the other side of your fear is your freedom"*

—JUMP

William Wallace, played by Mel Gibson in the movie *"Braveheart"*, one of my favorite movies, is faced with many fears and battles. After losing his wife, whom he had just barely married, he sets out to help the people of Scotland regain their land. He must jump through many layers of his own fear to the climax where he is beheaded, and his last word to his friends and people who battled with him was "Freedom."

The Freedom jump is perhaps the jump that we must take each day. Fear is always a clear and present danger and must be acknowledged and then put in a bag. This must be why in the passages of the Good Book the Lord God says to His people, us, "Fear not" 365 days. Is that a coincidence? I believe it is a beautiful gift from God to warn us that we will experience daily fears, but jump to freedom each of the 365 days I have given you each year to live, and jump into the mysteries of life.

Remember in the Indiana Jones movie where Indiana Jones, played by Harrison Ford, is at the base of a tall cave, mountain, high in the sky, and he must cross a chasm to get to the other mountain so he can pursue the chalice, the Cup of Life? He steps out with one foot in the air, nothing below him, but, as he does, a beautiful crystal walkway appears to catch his foot and allows him to cross over to the other side to pursue his destiny.

When you come to the edge of all the light you know, and are about to jump into the darkness of the unknown, faith is knowing one of two things will happen. There will be something solid to stand on, or you will be taught to fly.

Every single day we must take the Geronimo Freedom Jump and yell "freedom" at the top of our lungs as William Wallace did, or be in total silence with, sometimes, our eyes closed, and take the leap. Each day the winds and waves will bring our fears to light but we, by faith, can choose to jump – again, not just for ourselves, but so others may break through their own fears. Together we grow stronger in our purpose, stronger in our passion, stronger in our pursuit of what this life has waiting us.

We all are the same, as my mentor, Bill Bailey said. We all have the same fears, doubts, and longings in life. Fear is a constant enemy that we must daily defeat. Fear always whispers, "not you, it can't be done, just wait until tomorrow, next week, next year." Then, guess what? You wake up as the Pink Floyd song says "10 years later," not knowing where it all went. Fear will keep you in your comfort zone. Fear will just keep saying, who are you to go for that, pursue this, start your own company, write that book, get married, raise a family, stand for a cause, live your values, even though they laugh at you. Fear God not man, the Bible says. Why do you think that is? Most people don't know those words are in there. It is to give us hope – when the words say "fear God," it does not mean tremble or be scared, or run into your closet. God's fear is love – if you are in awe of Me, and know I am greater than men, then know I walk with you daily. As Psalms 118:6 says, "The Lord is on my side. I will not be afraid. What can man do to me? What do you have to fear? – Call on Me." Take the Geronimo Jump and fear will disappear; it will be put where it belongs in an empty place. Fear can never produce light. Fear paralyzes, keeps us numb, keeps our light on the dimmest setting so we won't shine.

When my two children, Brandon and Sophia, were about 10 and 8 years old, I put their pictures in a frame with the words of Nelson Mandela in the inaugural speech he gave in 1994. I sat them both down and spoke the words by using their names, and then hung the frames in their shared bathroom so that they would be the first and last thing they read each day. At first, I don't think they understood the impact of the message, yet I believed that the words would give them courage and strength to one day take Geronimo jumps.

Read and take these words in for your life:

*Our deepest fear is not that we are inadequate. Our deepest fear is that we are powerful beyond measure. It is our light, not our darkness that most frightens us. We ask ourselves, who am I to be brilliant, gorgeous, talented and fabulous? Actually, who are you not to be? You are a child of god. Your playing small doesn't serve the world. There's nothing enlightened about shrinking so that other people around you won't feel insecure around you. We are born to make manifest the glory of God that is within us. It's not just in some of us, it's in everyone. And as we let our own light shine, we unconsciously give others permission to do the same. As we are liberated from our own fear, our presence automatically liberates others.*

My hope is, that if you get just one thing out of this book, you believe those words about you. Take these words by Mandela, read them daily, memorize them so when that doubt rises, and when that fear comes, when it whispers to you, speak these words aloud and know them to be true so you might then come to rise and to lift others, to face your fears. Speaking words of life to yourself and others is one of the greatest jumps you can do each day. Yes, it is a battle, daily, but knowing this and embracing it fully will ensure it is no surprise when fear awakens you in the morning and tries to go to sleep with you in the evening.

Let's end this chapter with something the Great Plains warriors would say to their sons first thing in the morning: "It's a good day to do great things."

In all the great legends, the hero, female or male, Joan of Arc or Martin Luther King, almost always was an ordinary man or woman with at least one tragic flaw – usually many. Nearly all people who attempt Geronimo Jumps, whether large or small, have made mistakes.

Take Winston Churchill, one of the most famous men to hail from England. Churchill, Prime Minister in WWII, led the allies to victory. However, once Churchill deliberately diverted food from India to feed Europeans at a time when India desperately needed it, worsening one of the cruelest famines in the country's history, leading to the deaths of over 3 million people.

Martin Luther King Jr., the Baptist minister and activist orator unlike anyone had ever heard before, was the face of the Civil Rights movement and one of the most respected men in history. But about his personal life? For starters, King allegedly plagiarized parts of his doctoral thesis on Systemic Theology.

And John Lennon, who wrote about peace and love, took the Beatles band to extraordinary levels. But Lennon had a dark side. He was abusive to his first wife and explored numerous affairs throughout his life.

Like any of us, these esteemed leaders weren't perfect, but they were willing and able to focus on their quest. Usually the goal was beyond their known abilities – and often the next goal was to encounter God, although the hero never knew this until the end.

If we can't say, each day, it is a good day to do great things, we will not experience a supercalifragilisticexpialidocious life. We need this kind of inspiration, desire or expectation. We can receive this from other men and women and also give it to others, somehow, unknowingly. We need to allow our souls to be stirred by some magnificent ambition, something that makes us jump out of bed in the morning, that calls us to be the hero of our own kind of story, even if we know we have more than one tragic flaw.

What is calling to the heroic within you? Let's take a jump into chapter three as we take the Hero's Journey Jump into Greatness.

# FREEDOM JUMP

## JUMPING CALLS TO ACTION

- List your fears. Be vulnerable. Remember you don't have to be strong, just connected to what is. What are the strong actions you can take to help you break your fears so you can begin to become more free?

- Copy and paste the words of Nelson Mandela in this chapter and carry them in your wallet or purse. Tape them on your mirror. Remind yourself that you are powerful beyond measure.

- Wherever you are in life, today is a good day to do great things. Maybe the great thing is to make someone a cup of coffee. Don't neglect the small things in life. They add up! Jump-start your day each day. List 5 things you can do today.

# GERONIMO JUMP 3

---

# HERO'S
# JOURNEY JUMP

*"We are not on our journey to save the world but to save*
*ourselves. But in doing that, you save the world.*
*The influence of a vital person vitalizes."*

—JOSEPH CAMPBELL

Many of you are possibly familiar with Joseph Campbell's work on the Hero's Journey. He has many writings on the Hero within, the Hero with a thousand faces. For our Hero's Journey Jump into living a supercalifragilisticexpialidocious life it cannot, I believe, be possible without looking at the work of Campbell, his Hero's Journey model and the jumps we have to make in each stage. If you can begin to even become aware of this and teach it to your children, it will be a powerful series of jumps that, if not taken, will lead to a life of mediocrity and despair.

I think T.S. Elliot summed up the Hero's Journeys we are about to jump into with these words:

> *"Happiness lies not in mindless hedonism, but in mindful challenge; not in having unlimited opportunities, but in focused possibilities; not in self-absorption, but in absorption of the world; not in having it done for you, but in doing it yourself. The unexamined life may not be worth living, but the unlived life is not worth examining."*

We can sit at the edge and watch things happen. We can stop things from happening. Or we can be in a position of always asking. Jump time, Geronimo time. Time to jump into a supercalifragilisticexpialidocious life. The Hero's Journey shows us the steps to begin living our Heroic Jump into the unknown. And that unknown determines our destiny.

The Hero's Journey Jump shows us that path to destiny, greatness, purpose, what lights our fire. This third jump will challenge us, grow us, deepen us into the man or woman we are called to be in this circle of life.

## STAGES OF THE HERO'S JOURNEY

There are twelve stages in the hero's journey. According to the Oracle Education Foundation Library, those stages are as follows:

1. **Ordinary World:** This stage refers to the hero's normal life at the start of the story, before the adventure begins.
2. **Call to Adventure:** The hero is faced with something that makes him begin his adventure. This might be a problem or a challenge he needs to overcome.
3. **Refusal of the Call:** The hero attempts to refuse the adventure because he is afraid.
4. **Meeting with the Mentor:** The hero encounters someone who can give him advice and ready him for the journey ahead.
5. **Crossing the First Threshold:** The hero leaves his ordinary world for the first time and crosses the threshold into adventure.
6. **Tests, Allies, Enemies:** The hero learns the rules of his new world. During this time, he endures tests of strength, of will, meets friends, and comes face to face with foes.
7. **Approach:** Setbacks occur, sometimes causing the hero to try a new approach or adopt new ideas.
8. **Ordeal:** The hero experiences a major hurdle or obstacle, such as a life or death crisis.
9. **Reward:** After surviving, the hero earns his reward or accomplishes his goal.
10. **The Road Back:** The hero begins his journey back to his ordi- nary life.
11. **Resurrection Hero:** The hero faces a final test where everything is at stake and he must use everything he has learned.
12. **Return with Elixir:** The hero brings his knowledge or the "elixir" back to the ordinary world, where he applies it to help all who remain.

As you can see, the Hero's Journey Model has 12 stages – similar but not the same as the 12 steps program of AA. The Hero's Journey combines all your physical, mental, emotional and spiritual components. It must, if we are to become whole, to be- come who we are capable of becoming. Bill Bailey, once said to me, "Mark, I don't see people as they are, I see them as what they can become."

The Hero's Journey Jump is this leap to having a supercalifragilis-ticexpialidocious life and it is not just one jump, it is series of jumps. It's like the lyrics in the **Jump** song by Van Halen:

*Might as well jump. Jump!*
*Go ahead and jump. Jump!*
*Get it in, jump. Jump!*
*Go ahead and jump.*
*Jump!*
*Jump!*
*Jump!*
*Jump!*

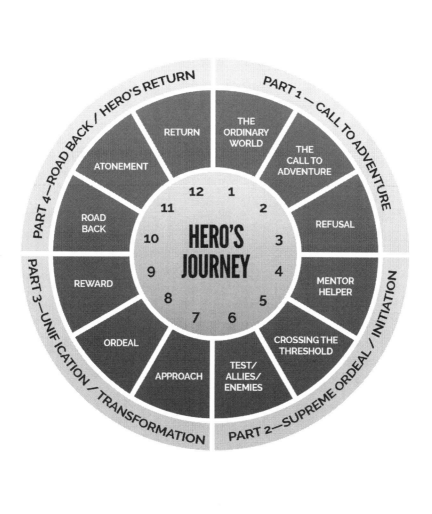

So, Van Halen had it correct. If you want a great life, you are go- ing to have to jump! Jump! Jump!

To illustrate the Hero's Journey for an idea on how the stages of the model work, I'm going to share a story about my son, Brandon. Brandon grew up in a small town with me, my wife, and daughter. Our town only had 70,000 people, and it was in the mountains of Medford, Oregon, 35 miles from the border of California. Until a high school trip to Washington D.C., Brandon never really ventured out of that small town. Then this trip opened his eyes to another world. The Capitol, the energy, the people, places, history, I believe, inspired him to see what is out there. It made him begin to wonder, what does the world mean to me? What's my place, my purpose, my passion? Experiencing history such as the Lincoln statue and the words were especially meaningful because Brandon was born on Abraham Lincoln's birthday, February 12.

## PART 1 — THE CALL TO ADVENTURE

This experience outside the world as he had always known it, set the stage for Part 1: the Call to Adventure – the call to jump, leap. To leave the ordinary world, the world of Medford, Oregon, not because it is bad, but to awaken another world. The call to adventure is within all of us, not just some. Whether we answer that call or not will greatly impact our purpose, our emotional and spiritual growth, our maturity, and our deepness in life. This is not a jump to take lightly. This jump to adventure will provide new meaning, new discoveries, new possibilities that, if not taken, will diminish the light in our life and the light we can bring to others.

As a young boy, Brandon always talked about a desire to move to the Big Apple – NYC one day. I think this desire might have been later reinforced by the Washington, D.C. trip, the appeal of a big city with a lot of history and lore. So when it came time for high school graduation, it was a big decision: stay in Medford where it is comfortable where you know everyone and life is predictable – or jump to a completely new adventure, new city, a new life! Brandon went back and forth on taking the jump. His friends called him advising him to stay, but the Hero's Adventure kept calling him to jump. There is always the refusal in this first stage of the Hero's Journey. Know this in life. When you're about to jump, and say yes, there's a tug back, a silent voice saying, "no way, you can't make that jump, it's too big, too wide, and you are not ready to make it there." Even your closest friends and family will discourage you from jumping, from taking the Hero's Adventure. Why is this? It is just human nature. We fear. We doubt. As Shakespeare said "doubts make traitors of us all."

Brandon hemmed and hawed, but in the end, he decided to push past the refusal stage and jump without knowing even one person in New York City.

The Hero's Journey is usually a jump that we make alone. It is a courage Jump and it comes from within. We all have it, but the question is, will we jump? Will we accept the call to Adventure? Brandon did. So, his journey continues into the next phase.

## PART 2 — THE SUPREME ORDEAL.

Brandon leaves the small town of Medford, 70,000 people, and goes into the heart of NYC – Manhattan – which has 70,000 x 10 people. He goes from mountains and rivers to city lights, sky-scrapers, now a 24/7 New World.

Once you seek a new land, mentors will come into your path. So, Brandon met helpers, guides, and people he would have never met if he'd not leaped. These people were there to help him stretch, give him new perspectives, and challenge his thinking as well as his values and beliefs. This is where in the journey the tests of strength, tests of will, occur. Challenges come into place, either strengthening your jump – or retreating into self-doubt and fear. You ask yourself, do I have what it takes?

## PART 3 — THE TRANSFORMATION

Part 3 of the Hero's Journey is the transformation phase, the approach, ordeal, or reward. In the approach, setbacks occur, causing the Hero/Jumper to try a new approach, adapt a new way. Brandon had to adapt to a New World in NYC with no car and no friends. This was new and unchartered territory. There were tall buildings, noisy taxies, and crowded subway stations – all calling for a different approach to living on your own thousands of miles from home. The ordeal requires facing your own obstacles and crisis of identity. Brandon had to discover "who am I?" Should I stay with safe, preconceived ways of being brought up, or should I take a risk and seek new goals and discoveries? New ideas and opportunity is where the rewards come in. This is for all of us, no risk, no reward.

Joseph Campbell once went on the Hero's Adventure Journey:

*"Furthermore, we have not even to risk the adventure alone, for the heroes of all time have gone before us. The labyrinth is thoroughly known. We have only to follow the thread of the hero path, and where we had thought to find an abomination, we shall find a god. And where we had thought to slay another, we shall slay ourselves, and where we had thought to travel outward, we will come to the center of our own existence. And where we had thought to be alone, we will be with all the world."*

— JOSEPH CAMPBELL

## PART 4 — THE ROAD BACK/HERO'S RETURN.

This is the transformation. When we jump into a new adventure, or take a different path, we experience new ideas, new insights, and growth. The atonement phase, or resurrection, is a jump that requires us to apply everything we have learned so far to start again. After two years in NYC, Brandon decided to move to Arizona, where we, as a family, had moved back to when he was in New York.

These next phases involve the Hero/Jumper, Brandon, bringing his knowledge or "the Elixir" (the gift) back to the ordinary world. This is also where he will apply it to help all who remain.

In Brandon's return, his gift of new knowledge helped our family in new ways we never thought possible. His jump enabled him to discover new ways of thinking, communicating, and living so that not only he could become stronger, but he could help his family grow as well. He gifted us the strength to take the jumps we needed to take so we all could live this supercalifragilisticexpialidocious life.

I will pause here and share a quote from Henry David Thoreau. We might all want to consider and embrace these words in our minds and hearts, over and over:

*"If one advances confidently in the direction of his dreams, and endeavors to live the life which he has imagined, he will meet with a success unexpected in common hours. He will pass an invisible boundary; new, universal, and more liberal laws will begin to establish themselves around and within him; and he will live with the license of a higher order of beings."*

— HENRY DAVID THOREAU

# HERO'S JOURNEY JUMP

## JUMPING CALLS TO ACTION

- Consider three adventures you would like to pursue. Remember, there is something magical when you take a pen or pencil and write those with your hand. You unknowingly go from your hand to your head to your heart.

- Today, and each day, try something new. Whether it's a new restaurant, a new route to work, a new trail to hike, or reaching out to someone not in your inner circle. Read a book. Call an old friend. Visit a new place.

- YouTube or Google a movie that inspires you or a person that took heroic actions in life. They're all around us each day. Even in the tragedies in life, the hero can emerge in the darkest hours.

- Consider or find five people who are moving forward, who are positive influencers. Meet with each one of them at least once a month over coffee, or exchange a phone call or email. Choose wisely.

## GERONIMO JUMP 4

---

# JERRY MAGUIRE JUMP

*"Failure to Jump is failing to live."*

—MARK BATTIATO

No, this is not the "show me the money" jump. This Jerry Ma- guire Jump, and the seven consecutive jumps that Jerry made in the movie, are significant enough for us to consider integrating in to our lives as well. If you have seen this movie, you might not have thought about how powerful the story was; or if you have not seen it, I recommend you rent this great movie and be prepared to be inspired. If you watch it again, or for the first time, keep this outline handy so you can see these truths come to life.

The inner jumps Jerry makes are about integrity, sincerity, spirit, empathy, vision, inspiration, and risk taking.

## INTEGRITY

"[Jerry Maguire] is a whole person" says author, musician, and business consultant Michael Jones, who wrote "Creating an Imaginative Life" (Conari Press, 1995). People [may] live with less money, but they will no longer have to compromise their integrity." It took personal integrity for Jerry to put his job on the line by speaking the truth in his mission statement. But he did so because he felt the need to integrate his personal values with his work values.

## SINCERITY

It is not until Jerry breaks down and speaks di- rectly and honestly to his sole client, the less-than-superstar football player, Rod Tidwell, that he is able to make a real connection with him. He advises the underrated athlete to get the chip off his shoulder and get back to his passion for the sport. Once Jerry and Rod really begin to communicate, both characters are able to move ahead and achieve success. "There is no connecting if there is no sincerity," says Allen Cox, author of "Redefining Corporate Soul, Linking Purpose & People" (Irwin, 1996).

## SPIRIT

Jerry is all spirit. He follows his vision, and even when he has moments of doubt, he looks to others for inspiration. "If we don't recognize the idea of spirituality in people, if that is not available, we can't push and prod and mold the world [or business] to change," says Margaret J. Wheatley, author of "A simpler Way" (Berrett-Koehler, 1996). "Most of my work deals with people reconnecting with what brought them into their work. It's what makes us human." Adds Barry Heermann, author of "Building Team Spirit" (McGraw-Hill, 1997) "forming team members refer to an energy dimension of the spirit that is beyond words. They produce extraordinary results. Miracles do happen."

## EMPATHY

"If a pitcher calls in his second or third season and says, 'I can't perform. I can't throw a fast ball. I quit. I've lost it,'" says Scott Boaras, baseball sports agent and owner of Scott Bo- aras Law Corporation, "you better know how to talk to that player and help that player obtain his greatest goals." You can't do that, however, unless you have the ability to put yourself in the other person's shoes. Jerry is able to understand what motivates his client and thereby helps him help himself.

## VISION

Jerry can see the whole picture and the quality is rare. "It's not just about the money," says Ralph Cindrich, a sports agent who represents about 50 NFL players. "It's the whole repre- sentative process. I have to match what the clubs' needs are with the dreams, goals, and quality of living the player seeks." (Sounds like a familiar human resource task.)

## INSPIRATION

Dorothy Boyd, the young accountant who is supporting a child alone, quits her stable, presumably well-paying job to join a "shaky" startup with Jerry Maguire because she was inspired by his "memo." How many managers do you know who truly inspire?

## RISK TAKING

Will Rogers once said that leaders go "out on the limb because that's where the fruit is." Risk takers are trailblazers, and once the path is trodden, others follow. Jerry does suffer some doubt after he goes out on a limb, but he holds on to his convictions and shows his client that it isn't just about money. In the end, Jerry helps Rod regain his passion for the sport, and the money does follow.

You will discover in life, that these mini jumps of empathy, vision, risk-taking, etc. are phases of a maturity development process. Those of us who choose not to develop deeper in these jumps remain bound in a life of mediocrity with less meaning, purpose, and truth – truth about ourselves, and others, willingness or ability to be truthful with us. You see Jerry's growth from the beginning to the end because he is willing to jump into these areas and become more of who he is supposed to be for himself, others, and life.

Someone once said, "most people are anxious to improve their lives, but unwilling to improve themselves, therefore they remain bound." You could substitute "unwilling to jump," therefore they cannot experience the highs and lows of life.

Just to be clear, crystal clear – jumping does not always produce highs in life – jumping can produce deep lows, depth, and introspection that can cause deep, deep pain, but also rediscov- ery into who you are and what you can become.

Leo Buscaglia, who wrote some great books you might want to look up on Amazon, said this once about life:

*"The gospel of St. John tells us that our house has many rooms, each with its own wonders to disclose. How can we be content to let spiders, rats, decay, and death take over our house?*

*"What may be is always potential for discovery. It's never too late. This knowledge should give man/woman his greatest challenge – the pursuit of self over our own personal Odyssey; discovering our rooms and putting them in order. It should challenge us not only to be a good person, a loving person, a feeling person, an intelligent person, but the best, most loving, feeling, intelligent person we are capable of. Our search is not in competition with any one else's. It becomes our own personal challenge."*

—LEO BUSCAGLIA

Remember, "where you stumble and fall, there you will find gold."

One last comment on Jerry Maguire's inner jumps – risk-taking: I'm very connected to this one and I would like to share something personal to this jump.

When I was about 27, I started a small health club promotional company. I moved to Atlanta, Georgia and worked with a health club chain called "Sports Life." I incorporated a direct marketing campaign with three clubs over about a year. I hired over 50 people, even convinced my brother, Victor, to quit his good-paying job with Sprint Company in Chicago, where he was a manager, to join me to expand. There were a lot of risks/jumps for both me and the people I encouraged to leap as well. That, or course, can be good or bad. Three months after my brother moved, we experienced a major drop in our marketing campaign and I had to let everyone go, including my brother. Needless to say, my parents were not too happy with me convincing my brother to jump in with me and then see the whole thing collapse in three short months. I remember after that, I was lost, not only emotionally, but I hardly had any money saved. I had no job, no purpose, and no vision of what to do next.

I moved back to Arizona and in with a friend. I owed a lot of money – close to $70,000 in debt. Twenty-five thousand of this was a loan my parents gave me. I remember calling my dad, who was a CPA in Chicago, and asked him if he could help me file chapter 7, 11 or 13. I knew those numbers, but just didn't know what they meant. I recall my dad, Lou, saying, "Son, I wish I could help you, but you need to pay back all of your debts," – and then a pause – "and you need to pay your mother and me the $25,000 we gave you as well." I didn't know what to say. My dad was not angry, nor did he even express disappointment in me, he just said it would be best for me to take responsibility for my decisions and not file bankruptcy. Of course, I didn't think that, I just wanted the quick "jump" out of it so I could say supercalifragilisticexpialidocious. But in the end, I agreed.

Well, it took five years to just get a payment to Dad. I remember during those five years I was fairly depressed. I couldn't sleep much. Bill collectors were calling all the time. I felt lost, sometimes even thinking I should check out of life. The girl I thought I would marry left me and I was slowly withering away mentally, physically, spiritually, and emotionally.

One day I remember going to the mailbox expecting more bill collection notices, and there was a package in the mail and in it was a poem from my Dad. It was called "Dare to Risk." My Dad just wrote a small note saying, "Mark, remember to keep risking."

## DARE TO RISK

*To laugh is to risk appearing the fool. To weep is to risk appearing sentimental.*

*To reach for another is to risk involvement.*

*To expose your ideas, your dreams, before a crowd is to risk their loss.*

*To love is to risk not being loved in return.*

*To live is to risk dying.*

*To believe is to risk failure.*

*But risks must be taken, because the greatest hazard in life is to risk nothing.*

*The people who risk nothing, do nothing, have nothing, are nothing.*

*They may avoid suffering and sorrow, but they cannot learn, feel, change, grow, love, live.*

*Chained by their attitudes, they are slaves; they have forfeited their freedom.*

*Only a person who risks is free.*
— AUTHOR UNKNOWN

As I read this, I couldn't believe my Dad knew exactly what words I needed to hear – not only to pick up the pieces, but risk again – to jump again, leap from a life that I was drowning in. For over 25 years,

I have carried that "Risk It" poem in my wallet. I hope that at least one person reading this will be encouraged to change the course of their life if that is what is needed to reclaim a purpose. Keep risking, my friend. Keep jumping. We all have lost love, hope, money, lost self-worth, or even our way. Come back. Jump again. Risk.

Risk is a choice rather than a fate — the actions we dare to take, which depend on how free we are to make choices.

We all must continue to jump — to keep risking and jump with all our heart, mind and soul. Watch, wait, and see the miracles that take place.

All things come together in their time if we continue to "Jump". The day I finished writing the last chapter of this book and literally sent it off to get typewritten, this blog from Seth Godin, whom I read almost daily (and highly recommend you subscribe to), was in my email. It was January 5th, 2019. The Spiderman Paradox. As Seth writes, just like Spiderman, we must not sit and watch another video; instead we must continue to jump like Spiderman. We must use our own great power for good.

## THE SPIDERMAN PARADOX

*On one hand, Uncle Ben's rule makes great sense: "With great power comes great responsibility."*

*The essence of the rule is that once you have great power, you need to take the responsibility that goes with it.*

*And yet, it's backfiring.*

*It's backfiring because so many walk away from their great power. They walk away because they don't want the responsibility.*

*We have the power to vote, but decide to stay home and whine.*

*The power to publish, but click instead.*

*The power to lead, but follow meekly.*

*The power to innovate, but ask for rules of thumb instead. The power to lend a hand, but walk away.*

*Most people watch videos, they don't make them. Most people read tweets, they don't write them. Most people walk away from the chance to lead online and off, in our virtual communities and with the people down the street.*

*In a democracy, we each have more power to speak up and to connect than we imagine. But most people don't publish their best work or seek to organize people who care. Most of the time, it's far easier to avert our eyes or blame the system or the tech or the dominant power structure.*

*There are millions who insist we'd be better off with a monarchy. The main reason: what happens after that is no longer their responsibility. Go work for the man, it saves you from having to be responsible.*

*When the local business disappears, it's because we didn't shop there. When the local arts program fades away, it's because we watched Netflix instead. And when the local school persists in churning out barely competent cogs for the industrial system, it's because we didn't speak up.*

*Culture is what we build, and that's powerful.*
—SETH GODIN

# JERRY MAGUIRE JUMP

## JUMPING CALLS TO ACTION

- Write one risk you need to jump into. Maybe it's just knowing you're on this earth for a purpose.

- Stay up late at night or get up at 3:00 am and write your mission for your life.

- Netflix the Jerry Maguire movie and get a notebook or your jour- nal to write the scenes down that touch your heart. That's most likely where your mission lies. Remember if you search, it will be revealed.

- Keep risking. Read the words from the Risk it poem. Only a per- son who risks is free!

# GERONIMO JUMP 5

---

# TRIFECTA JUMP

*"All great things come in threes"*

*"Two people are better off than one, for they can help each other succeed. If one person falls, the other can reach out and help. But someone who falls alone is in real trouble. Likewise, two people lying close together can keep each other warm. But how can one be warm alone? A person standing alone can be attacked and defeated, but two can stand back-to-back and conquer. Three are even better, for a triple-braided cord is not easily broken."*

—ECCLESIASTES 4:9-12

In 1992, British running athlete, Derek Redmond, was taking part in the 400 meters. Redmond had missed out on the team in 1988 by mere minutes. An injury caused him to have to withdraw and watch from the sidelines as Steve Lewis won the gold for the U.S. But that was in the past. By Barcelon in 1992, Derek was injury-free and determined to win a place on the podium. That wasn't something unfeasible; he had already shown he was no stranger to winning. The year before, he was part of the British 4 x 400-meter relay team that had won the gold at the World Championships. He was confident he could add to that success at the Olympics. His first heat was a solid run, with his quickest time in the last four years. A great start to the games! By the second heat, Derik was starting to find his groove. He won his heat again, and it looked like he still had plenty of gas left in the tank. Once it was time for the semi-finals, Derek was confident he would be racing in the 400-meter final. He just had to get through his last test. In Derek's words, "I had a great warm-up; stride and everything went well, came out on the track, put my blocks down, no problems, told us to strip down, stripped down. Then he has me a little bit where your standing in your lane and they come and shove a camera in your face so everyone can see who you are, blocked that out and everything. " He continued, "'On your mark, get set....' The race went well. I couldn't believe that I was running quick. It's hard to tell, positions in the 400-meter due to the staggering of the athletes." But Derek was holding his own, well within the time he would need to qualify for the final. Then it happened. Derek said, "the next thing I heard was a funny pop." He knew immediately that he was in trouble. The funny pop had been a hamstring tearing. A few more steps and he fell to the ground in agony. In severe pain, Derek could only hold his head in his hands as the other competitors sprinted to the finish line. He said, "I watched them go over the line, and obviously I knew it was over. Four years of hard work and waiting, and it was all over in the sot painful way possible." But Derek had not travelled all this way to not finish another race. The bitter memory of missing out in the Seoul had stayed with him. As medics came to help him off the track, Derek refused to go out without a fight. In spite of his excruciating pain, he was going to finish the race. But he didn't have to finish the race on his own. Breaking his way through the stands, came his father, Jim, desperate to help his son in any way he could. Derek struggled to embrace the man who had done so much for his career. The pain continued down the last 100 meters. Back in Derek's home town, Northampton, the sight of seeing her brother and father struggle so dramatically, sent Derek's pregnant sister into labor earlier than expected. In great agony, Derek was in a flood of tears as he finally crossed the line. The crown roared the man on. And while Redmond might have failed in his goal to win a medal, finishing the way he did made him an instant celebrity. The sight of Derek using his father as a crutch has become one of the most endearing Olympics images. Messages of support poured in from around the world, praising his sportsmanship and perseverance. It was the ultimate show of Olympic spirit. It was the ultimate jump. Despite the heartbreak, crossing the finish line proved you don't have to be a gold medalist to be a hero. The line so many of us have heard applies here: it's not how you start, it's how you finish.

In this story, you see that all great things come in three. The Olympic runner, Derek, his father coming to help him when his son fell to the ground, and the crowd cheering him on as he crossed the finish line.

The Trifecta Jump includes three inner jumps. Those three jumps for a life of giving, growth and grace. Let's think about giving. Most of us have heard the saying about "give to receive". The Bible talks about the tithe – giving back 10% of what you earn. I would say that most people agree it is good to give. Even God said, test me on this and see if I don't bless your life when you return a small amount back to me. So, why don't we give, or jump up to give more of our wealth away? Why don't we jump when charities ask for help? Or jump to help a lost person on the street asking us to give, even if just a dollar? The Giving Jump is part of the Trifecta in life. Why is this jump so difficult? I believe there are two reasons.

First, and you might not like this one, it's selfishness. I'm still working on this myself and will probably continue until the day I die. We are selfish and want to keep it all to ourselves out of not having enough. In giving, we give a little bit of our selfishness away. To make it a daily habit to put others' needs before our own is a continuous effort in humility and generosity. But if we give from the heart, we can experience a small taste of winning the Trifecta each day we live.

The second reason we don't give has to do with TRUST. Trust that what we give will come back if not literally in the form of spiritual reward. God says what you give you will receive. When we don't give in life daily, we don't trust God to truly provide. We doubt, we have fear, and insecurities.

So, when we give of our money, time, and service, or volunteer in whatever way and not seek first ourselves, but seek the higher path, it will always come back. In the Good Book, it says, it will come back one hundred fold. If we truly trust and believe this, we would be winning the Trifecta daily. Think about this. Be a go-giver. Go and give in whatever way you can. Jump the next time someone asks you to give of your time, money and resources. Do not fear; God says, don't I take care of even the sparrows who fly?

Jim Rohn, said once, "money only makes you more of what you are. So, if you're greedy [about] money, more money will make you greedier. If you are a giver, the more wealth you make, the more you will just give." "Money is just energy," Joseph Campbell said. What kind of energy are you giving of daily? The more energy you release in the world to do good, the more energy you will receive. Whenever I give some money to someone on the street or serve at a shelter to feed families, I always, always feel energized. I feel more alive because I could give something of myself that is greater. A jump to give in any way to others will revitalize your purpose in this world. It's certainly been true for me.

The more you give to others in little ways, the more you receive. Give five minutes to phone your Mom, Dad, a friend, or someone hurting. Visit someone in the hospital. Serve food to those who are hungry. Give of your time. Give and receive. Believe this. Jump into giving the next time the opportunity or motivation calls. Rise up to a supercalifragilisticexpialidocious life – a life of great calling.

Let's move to the second part of the Trifecta: Growth. Bill Bailey, who grew up in Kentucky with 13 siblings, coined the phrase, "your Growth into Greatness." Growth is a constant jump if you choose to live a life of greatness. "If you're not growing, you are dying," said George Land, the author of the book "Grow or Die." How do you continue to grow? Rohn gave a single answer in his lectures around the world. Read books, hang around people who know more than you and keep taking the courses, the seminars, the Ted talks. Just show up, he said, and you will be amazed.

Jim used to say, "for heaven's sake, when you die, don't leave your 84-inch LED TV to your kids. Leave your library, your books, your Geronimo knowledge, your journals, the book you wrote." "Miss a meal," Jim said, "but don't miss a book!" (See the supercalifragilisticexpialidocious book list for jumping in the back of this book.)

One idea from a book can change your life. That's how you grow. Hang around people who know more than you. Don't be ashamed, or embarrassed. We all have gifts and some people are more gifted in areas or growth than we are. Hang around them. Learn, grow, become! Jump!

My daughter, Sophia, (which means "wisdom") has taught me how to laugh again. She knows how to make people feel comfortable, be themselves, to let their guard down. She has the gift of joy.

That's something to be around. It's contagious. Just last night, as I write this, we all watched the last Jurassic Park movie. When it was over, she started making sounds like a raptor. We all were laughing. She was laughing the hardest and crying at the same time. That's growth. The ability to laugh at yourself and not be so serious shows growth. Seriously, life is not to be so serious, sad and solemn. To laugh is one of the greatest gifts you can give others. Sophia has rekindled that in me again for I can be introspective and too absorbed in my thoughts to enjoy the moment. There was a season in my life in which my marriage was going through some trials. The reasons this was happening was not important but it was a time of deep sorrow, pain, and unhappiness. During this rough time, Sophia could still light up the room with her smile, while playing a song and dancing, or jumping in my lap and giving me a hug and kiss. She would light my spirit to keep moving forward day by day.

Sophia has a natural knack for making others feel accepted. What a touch from Heaven, and what a gift she has been to our family. She has made all of us jump into the beauty of laughter and to be spontaneous in her joy and love. I love being around that girl. If God allows her to be a mother someday, what a great childhood those kids will have. There will be a lot of laughter and joy in that home. That's why Jim Rohn said one of the keys to continual growth is to hang around people who are growing, whether in sports, academics, their spiritual life, business, marriage or the school of life in general. A friend of mine, Jim Breeze, said to me when our kids were in high school and troubles came, whether it be drugs, or grades or sports team disappointments, he would share with his kids these words to make them, hopefully, think and reflect: "show me your friends and I will show you your future." Wise words for growth. Show me people you hang out with and it will show you how far you jump in life. Your growth, your jumps in life, will be critical to the people you are around. Sometimes the best jumps you will make, and the most difficult, will be jumping out of bad relationships, friends who are taking you down a sad path, – unhealthy emotional relationships. Jump out of those and jump into ones that offer hope, good words for you, encouragement – who tell you you've got what it takes. Jump away from the takers and jump to the givers. There are plenty of both. Jump to the givers and your life will be so much more free and worthwhile. Make the most valuable gift in this life - choose wisely.

And finally, Grace – the last jump in the Trifecta Jump in leading a supercalifragilisticexpialidocious life. Grace is received and can't be earned. In my life, I have received Grace too many times to count. Grace is a gift from God and others who give compassion, who offer freely to you without expecting anything in return. Grace is a beautiful gift we can only give to ourselves for all the mistakes we have made, words wewe want to take back, or actions we wished we hadn't done and would like to retract. Grace gives us the chance to press RESET; to restore ourselves and others. Being Grace, receiving Grace, becoming Grace in your life is a beautiful jump to keep on jumping into.

Many of you know the lead singer of U2, Bono, who wrote this incredible song and lyrics to the Grace Jump. YouTube and play the song every day - it will be worth it if it helps you grow more in Grace. Grace makes beauty out of ugly things.

## GRACE

*Grace, she takes the blame*
*She covers the shame*
*Removes the stain*
*It could be her name*

*Grace, it's the name for a girl*
*It's also the thought that changed the world*
*And when she walks on the street*
*You can hear the strings*
*Grace finds goodness in everything*

*Grace, she's got the walk*
*Not on a ramp or on chalk*
*She's got the time to talk*
*She travels outside the karma*
*She travels outside the karma*
*When she goes to work*
*You can hear her strings*
*Grace finds beauty in everything*

*Grace, she carries a world on her hips*
*No champagne flute for her lips*
*No twirls or skips between her fingertips*

*She carries a pearl in perfect condition*
*What once was hurt*
*What once was friction*
*What left a mark*
*No longer stings*
*Because Grace makes beauty*
*Out of ugly things*

Grace makes beauty out of ugly things. The Grace Jump, I believe, as Bono writes "finds goodness in everything" because "Grace makes beauty out of ugly things." Wow.

To Jump into the discovery of what Grace can bring and give to our lives and others is a thought that truly did change the world. Grace is not just a thought but action we can give to bring more Grace into our words, actions, work, family, relationships. Be Grace and receive Grace. No better Jump to become more vital in our life than be a man or women after Grace. They said that King David in the Bible was a man after God's heart. Without Grace you cannot have a heart for God or others. Grace is vital to your heart and vital to the heartbeat of others.

That's the Trifecta Jump: Giving, Growth, Grace. A chord that is three strands strong.

# TRIFECTA JUMP

## JUMPING CALLS TO ACTION

- Give something away each week in your life. It could be money, your time to a cause, or just a smile to someone to brighten their day.

- Find out where your energy comes from. What activities destroy your mood or drain your energy? What activities make you feel good and give energy?

- Identify the 20% of activities that bring the most results for every aspect of your life. Focus on doing more of these activities that improve those.

- Continuously re-evaluate self-knowledge, this is where your growth will come. Get feedback from others. Feedback is the breakfast of champions.

- Extend grace to yourself daily. Start with yourself so you can give it to others. You cannot give away something without possessing it yourself. Grace makes everything beautiful.

*"A good plan today is better than a perfect plan tomorrow."*
GEORGE S. PATTON

*"Let us not grow weary in doing good, for in due season we shall reap a harvest if we do not give up."*
GALATIANS 6:9

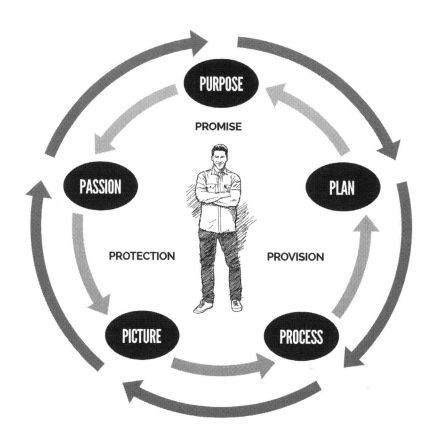

You have 2 choices: Profess your words or possess your actions. The Power comes not from professing words but from possessing them and saying, "I will do it." "I WILL JUMP." Only then will the promise, protection and provision begin again and again. Warning: the deadly "P" will come, PROCRASTINATION. This will lead to doubt, despair, and denial of what's possile in your life. Secret: Proclaim, Plant, and Purpose each day to pursue your Jump.

# GERONIMO JUMP 6

---

# EGO JUMP

*"We have met the enemy and he is us"*

—POGO BY WALT KELLY

The Ego Jump might be the most important Jump to make daily. Someone once said e-g-o stands for Edging God Out. Think about that for a moment. Reflect on that statement for your own life when you have taken matters into your own hands, in your own mind and have not paused to reflect. Ask God, Is this Thy will? Is this what you would like me to say? Is this the direction I should go? Pride before the fall, the book of Proverbs says. Ego will keep you falling into a never ending bottomless pit. You will end up in a dark place, lonely, confused, unsatisfied, no matter how successful you look on the outside to the world.

Jesus says humility is the key to a life – not thinking that you are God's gift to the world and everything revolves around you.

Coach John Wooden said to his basketball players over and over, "it's what you learn after you know it all that counts." If that quote does not humble you or make you stop and pause to look at yourself in the mirror and say, could I improve here? Can I be a better man/woman? Is my life deepening with others? Are my words bringing life or death?

Let's be truthful to ourselves. We all know deep within we could be more considerate, more compassionate, more loving, less critical, less angry, less demanding of ourselves and others!

A pastor once said from the pulpit "if you knew the past and story of others, you would have even compassion for the worst of men. Everyone is fighting a hard battle. Be kind. Listen. Be slow to judge, realizing you are one step away from falling again into the Ego Jump. This is why you should just ask your ego to leave. Ego is always with you, but you can take steps and follow principals to keep you on track.

Let's look at what Coach Wooden's father gave to his son, John, when he was a young boy. John Wooden credits his father for grounding him in the principles which he has based his life and career on.

> *"When I graduated from our little three-room grad school in Centerton, Indiana," says Wooden, "my father gave me a little card on which he had written out his creed." At the top of the card was written, "Seven Things to Do." They are:*
> *Be true to yourself. Help others.*
> *Make each day your masterpiece.*
> *Drink deeply from good books, especially the Bible.*
> *Make friendship a fine art.*
> *Build a shelter against a rainy day.*
> *Pray for guidance and count and give thanks for your blessings every day.*

Wooden remembers that all his father said to him when he handed him the card was, "Son, try and live up to these things." Wooden certainly did.

Wooden might be best known for his Pyramid of Success. He drilled it into his players over and over.

Basketball great Kareem Abdul-Jabbar, who played for Wooden, once told a reporter he thought the Pyramid was kind of corny when he first saw it, but he later realized that it had a great effect on his career and later life.

Wooden always maintained that the order and placement of each block was essential to the pyramid's success. Considering his success, who can contradict him?

## JOHN WOODEN'S
# PYRAMID OF SUCCESS

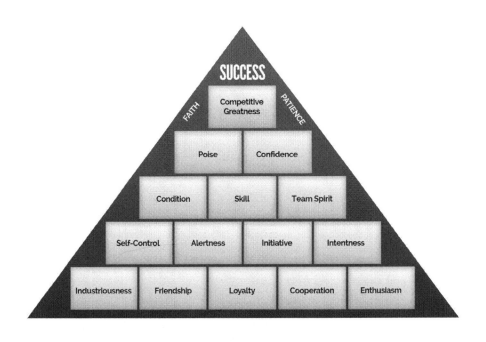

*"It's what you learn after you know it all that counts."*

—COACH JOHN WOODEN

What a lot of people might not know is that Wooden was a three-time All-American at Purdue University. "My coach at Purdue, Piggy Lambert, constantly reminded us: "The team that makes the most mistakes will probably win." That may sound a bit odd, but there is a great deal of truth in it. The doer makes mistakes. Coach Lambert taught me that mistakes come from doing, but so does success. The individual who is mistake-free is also probably sitting around doing nothing. And that's a very big mistake.

Like all great coaches and teachers, Wooden did not teach basketball. He taught life. If you learned a little basketball on the side, so much the better. Among my favorite Wooden quotes:

*"Develop a love for details. They usually accompany success."*
*"Failure is not fatal, but failure to change might be."*

**Mackay's Moral:** (courtesy of John Wooden)

*"Talent is God- given, be humble. Fame is man-given, be thankful. Conceit is self- given, be careful."*
— JOHN WOODEN

John Wooden's father said to his son, "Try to live up to these in life." I promise you, if you even focus on one of these principles by John's father, you will drive ego away each day and live a life that you will feel empowered by and help others to feel empowered as well. There is nothing better than empowering good values, a good heart, a good path and a good moral compass to guide your daily living.

James Allen, who wrote "As a Man Thinketh" said, "a man is literally what he thinks, his character being is the sum of his thoughts."

Bill Bailey once asked his co-workers, "would you like to know the secret to all of your problems and how to solve them?" He told them all to close their eyes. Then he placed a small mirror in front of them and said, "open your eyes, see, you are the problem and solution to all of your problems."

Be humble. Let go so others can come in. You know when you are not acting from ego when you don't need to hate. Be still, deal lovingly with what is in front of you. Stop the game of ego-comparison, competition, resentment, bitterness.

Individualism leads to eccentricity and annoyance. No man or woman is an island. We all need each other to create breakthroughs in our lives. My wife, Christy, says a breakdown is just the beginning of a breakthrough, a miracle in its first stage.

Let me leave this chapter with four ideas/thoughts – one is the credo by Thomas Gordon, PhD on his relationships with others; Coach Wooden's Pyramid of Success that you can study, live, practice and share with others and two poems about life.

*Remember, people are unreasonable, illogical and self-centered.*
**Love them anyway.**

*If you do good, people will accuse you of selfish ulterior motives.*
**Do good anyway.**

*If you're successful, you'll win false friends and make true enemies.*
**Try to succeed anyway.**

*Honesty and frankness will get you nowhere, they make you vulnerable.*
**Be honest and frank anyway.**

*People favor underdogs, but they follow the top dogs.*
**Fight for some underdogs anyway.**

*What you spend years building may be destroyed overnight.*
**Build anyway.**

*People really need help, but they attack you if you try to help them.*
**Try anyway.**

*Give the world the best you have and you'll get kicked in the mouth.*
**Give the world the best you have anyway.**

*You see, in the final analysis, it is between you and God.*
**It was never between you and THEM, anyway.**

—MOTHER TERESA

## A CREDO

FOR MY RELATIONSHIPS WITH OTHERS

*YOU and I are in [a] relationship which I value and want to keep. Yet each of us is a separate person with his own unique needs and the right to meet those needs.*

*When you are having problems meeting your needs, I will try to listen with genuine acceptance in order to facilitate your finding your own solutions instead of depending on mine. I also will try to respect your right to choose your own beliefs and developing your own values, different though they may be from mine.*

*However, when your behavior interferes with what I must do to get my own needs met, I will openly and honestly tell you how your behavior affects me, trusting that you will respect my needs and feelings enough to try to change the behavior that is unacceptable to me. Also, whenever some behavior of mine is unacceptable to you,*

*I hope that you will openly and honestly tell me your feelings. I will then listen and try to change my behavior.*

*At those times when we find that either of us cannot change his behavior to meet the other's needs, let us acknowledge that we have a conflict-of-needs that requires resolving. Let us then commit ourselves to resolve each such conflict without either of us resorting to the use of power or authority to try to win at the expense of the other losing. I respect your needs, but I also must respect my own.*

*So let us always strive to search for a solution that will be acceptable to both of us. Your needs will be met, but so will mine — neither will lose, both will win.*

*In this way, you can continue to develop as a person through satisfying your own needs, but so can I. Thus, ours can be a healthy relationship in which each of us can strive to become what he is capable of being. And we can continue to relate to each other with mutual respect, love and peace.*

—THOMAS GORDON, PHD

## THE GUY IN THE GLASS

AKA, THE MAN IN THE MIRROR

*When you get what you want in your struggle for self and the world makes you king for a day then go to the mirror and look at yourself and see what that man has to say.*

*For it isn't your father, mother or wife whose judgment upon you must pass, but the man whose verdict counts the most in your life is the one staring back from the glass.*

*He's the fellow to please, never mind all the rest. For he's with you right to the end, and you've passed your most difficult test if the man in the glass is your friend.*

*You may be like Jack Horner and "chisel" a plum, and think you're a wonderful guy, But the guy in the glass says you're only a bum. If you can't look him straight in the eye*

*You can fool the whole world, down the highway of years, and take pats on the back as you pass. But your final reward will be heartaches and tears if you've cheated the man in the glass.*

— DALE WEMBROW, 1934

# PYRAMID OF SUCCESS

## COMPETITIVE GREATNESS

"Perform at your best when your best is required. Your best is required each day."

## POISE

"Be yourself. Don't be thrown off by events whether good or bad."

## CONFIDENCE

"The strongest steel is well-founded self-belief. It is earned, not given."

## CONDITION

"Ability may get you to the top, but character keeps you there – mental, moral and physical."

## SKILL

"What a leader learns after you've learned it all counts most of all."

## TEAM SPIRIT

"The star of the team is the team. 'We' supersedes 'me'."

## SELF-CONTROL

"Control of your organization begins with control of yourself. Be disciplined."

## ALERTNESS

"Constantly be aware and observing. Always seek to improve yourself and the team."

## INITIATIVE

"Make a decision! Failure to act is often the biggest failure of all."

## INTENTNESS

"Stay the course. When thwarted try again; harder; smarter. Persevere relentlessly."

## INDUSTRIOUSNESS

"Success travels in the company of very hard work. There is no trick, no easy way."

## FRIENDSHIP

"Strive to build a team filled with camaraderie and respect: comrades-in-arms."

## LOYALTY

"Be true to yourself. Be true to those you lead."

## COOPERATION

"Have utmost concern for what's right rather than who's right."

## ENTHUSIASM

"Your energy and enjoyment, drive and dedication will stimulate and greatly inspire others."

# 12 LESSONS IN LEADERSHIP

1. Good Values Attract Good People

2. Love Is The Most Powerful Four-Letter Word

3. Call Yourself A Teacher

4. Emotion Is Your Enemy

5. It Takes 10 Hands To Make A Basket

6. Little Things Make Big Things Happen

7. Make Each Day Your Masterpiece

8. The Carrot Is Mightier Than A Stick

9. Make Greatness Attainable By All

10. Seek Significant Change

11. Don't Look At The Scoreboard

12. Adversity Is Your Asset

*"It's what you learn after you know it all that counts."*
—COACH JOHN WOODEN

*"Failure is not fatal, but failure to change might be."*
—COACH JOHN WOODEN

*"Make each day a masterpiece."*
—COACH JOHN WOODEN

# EGO JUMP

---

## JUMPING CALLS TO ACTION

- Seek and speak Truth. You can handle it. Be truthful each morning. Humble yourself and ask yourself what do I need to stop doing or start doing? Who do I need to tell, "I was wrong."

- Go for a drive in your car or go on a walk and listen to some podcasts or DVDs of great men or women who were humble, didn't brag on themselves (for example: Jim Rohn, Mother Teresa, John Wooden). Turn your car radio into a U.O.W. (University on Wheels.)

- Remember, it's what you learn after you know it all that counts. Learn one thing each day. Maybe it could be from a book, a ser- mon or a friend. Ask questions. You may realize there are "acres of diamonds" all around you.

- Beware of letting the ego tempt us to think: I'm the captain of my ship. I decide, I will, I create. I did it by myself. I did it my way." How can you do to avoid the temptation to take the helm alone?

# GERONIMO JUMP 7

---

# EPIC JUMP

*"Every jump is an entry somewhere else."*
—ANONYMOUS

*"This is your last chance — after this there is no turning back.
You take the blue pill, the story ends. You wake up in bed and
believe whatever you want to believe.*

*You take the red pill, you stay in wonderland — and I will show
you how deep the rabbit hole goes — remember — all I'm offering
is the truth — nothing more."*
—THE MATRIX - MORPHEUS TO NEO

Wonderland. What does that mean? Stay in Wonderland. Jim Rohn always said, stay curious in life. Stay in wonder.

To live the Epic Life, we must practice Wonder. In a world of "been there, done that" and "whatever" — wonder is often considered naive or un-hip. But, "wonder" is the root of "wonderful" and the beginning of the philosophical quest. Webster offers the following synonyms: admiration, appreciation, astonishment, reverence, surprise, amazement, awe.

> *"The Road goes on and on*
> *Down from the door where it began.*
> *Now far ahead the Road has gone,*
> *And I must follow if I can,*
> *Pursuing it with eager feet,*
> *Until it joins some larger way . . ."*
>
> —J.R.R. TOLKIEN

In one of his books, 'Epic: the Story God is Telling,' John Eldredge writes "we live in a far more dramatic, far more dangerous story than we ever imagined. The reason we love the 'Chronicles of Narnia', or 'Star Wars' or 'The Matrix' or the 'Lord of the Rings' is because they are telling us something about our lives that we never, ever get on the evening news or from most pulpits. They are reminding us of the epic we are created for." Why should we take the Epic Jump? Because, for all of us as John Eldredge summarizes, "something has been calling you all of your life. You've heard it on the wind and in the music you love, in laughter and in tears, and especially in the stories that have ever captured your heart. There is a secret written on your heart. A valiant hero-lover and his beloved. An Evil One and a great battle to fight. A journey and a quest more dangerous and more thrilling than you could imagine. A little Fellowship to see you through."

*"Open my eyes that I may see wonderful things."*

—PS 119:18 NIV

## TODAY, OPEN YOUR EYES

*One day Elisha and his servant awoke to find the house they were in surrounded by an army of enemy soldiers. His servant panicked and asked, "What are we going to do?" So Elisha prayed, "Lord, open his eyes so he may see." (2Ki 6:17 NIV). Suddenly he saw their enemies surrounded by an even bigger army of angels. On their way home to Emmaus, Cleopas and his companion were heartbroken because Jesus, the One in whom they'd placed their hopes, had been crucified and buried. Out of nowhere a stranger joined them on their journey, and when they reached home they invited him to stay for supper. As he prayed and pronounced a blessing over their meal, the eyes of Cleopas and his companion were opened and they recognized that the stranger was none other than Jesus Himself (See Lk 24:13-35). A man on a commuter train kept gazing out of the window and saying "Wonderful; just wonderful!" What was he looking at? Run-down apartment buildings and trash spilling over onto the sidewalk! After hearing him say "Wonderful" four or five times, the lady beside him remarked, "it doesn't look too wonderful to me." Whereupon the man replied, "I've been blind for the past thirty years. But through the skill of a surgeon, the generosity of a donor, and a corneal transplant, I've been given the gift of two new eyes. And, to me, everything I see is wonderful." Grumbling blinds you to God's blessings, but gratitude opens your eyes to enjoy them. So, today, ask the Lord to open your eyes to all the "wonderful things" that surround you.*

— JENTEZEN FRANKLIN

I truly believe if you want to live the Epic Life and live the supercalifragilisticexpialidocious life, you will need, at some time, to turn your heart and mind to the greatest epic story in history and become part of that story of Creation. Ask God to open your eyes to what is possible. Ask God what is your Epic calling. Maybe it's providing for a child in need across the globe that you have never met. Maybe it's giving your support to a cause that stirs in your heart. Maybe it is encouraging your wife, son, or daughter. Maybe it is to share or hear a dying person's last words, to hold someone's hand going through a hard season, or to be a "lid lifter" as John Maxwell says in his book "Leadership 101." To lift other lives is an Epic Jump. Every longing is a longing for God. Does that explain the longing you have in your heart for a life you haven't yet found? Most importantly without God's Holy Spirit giving you back to your heart, your true source of life and Epic Jump will just make a small splash. But with God, big ripples will continue on even after you leave this temporary life. So, why not ask God to give you the eyes to see what is possible for your Epic Story? Be humble, be disciplined, be expectant, be in wonder. Believe.

I've already shared with you my EPIC story. When I resigned from my father-in-law's company in Arizona and decided to more to Oregon when Christy wasn't working and our children were very young, as I mentioned earlier on, it was a jump. A leap of faith. We were moving to a new area with no family and friends, and I didn't have a future job or income. This was epic for all of us. At times it was humbling, other times it was exciting to see what would be revealed. Trusting in our Creator to provide for us in this Geronimo Jump into the unknown was a real test – traveling with just two used cars and a U-Haul with all we had. But we had each other and enough love, laughter, and belief that good things were ahead in a land where the trees where a little greener and the weather was a little cooler.

*"Remember, all positions in life are temporary, except one, God...let that give hope to the poor and caution to the rich."*
—WILLIAM E. BAILEY

I would be remiss not to again share the last few pages of John Eldredge's book "Epic," to remind us of the story God is telling – like every great story that echoes. It reminds us of these eternal truths that would be good to keep in mind as we take the next step out the door:

*"First, things are not what they seem.*

*Where would we be if Eve had recognized the serpent for who he really was? And that carpenter from Nazareth — he's not what he appears to be, either. There is far more going on around us than meets the eye. We live in a world with two halves, one part that we can see and another part that we cannot. We must live as though the unseen world (the rest of reality) is more weighty and more real and more dangerous than the part of reality we can see.*

*Second, we are at war.*

*This is a love Story, set in the midst of a life-and-death battle.*

*Just look around you. Look at all the casualties strewn across the field. The lost souls, the broken hearts, the captives. We must take this battle seriously. This is no child's game. This is war — a battle for the human heart.*

*Third, you have a crucial role to play. That is the third eternal truth spoken by every great story, and it happens to be the one we most desperately need if we are ever to understand our days. Frodo underestimated who he was. As did Neo. As did Wallace. As did Peter, James and John. It is a dangerous thing to underestimate your role in the Story. You will lose heart, and you will miss your cues.*

*This is our most desperate hour. You are needed.*

*We are now far into this Epic that every great story points to.*

*WE have reached the moment where we, too, must find our courage and rise up to recover our hearts and fight for the hearts of others. The hour is late, and much time has been wasted. Aslan is on the move; we must rally to him at the stone table. We must find Geppetto lost at sea. WE must ride hard, ride to Minas Tirith and join the last great battle for Middle Earth.*

*Jesus calls to you to be his intimate ally once more. There are great things to be done and great sacrifices to be made. You won't lose heart if you know what's really going on here, where this Story is headed and what your Lover has promised you.*

*It is a world of magic and mystery, of deep darkness and flickering starlight. It is a world where terrible things happen and wonderful things, too. It is a world where godliness is pitted against evil, love against hate, order against chaos, in a great struggle where often it is hard to be sure who belongs to which side because appearances are endlessly deceptive. Yet for all its confusion and wildness, it is a world where the battle goes ultimately to the good, who live happily ever after, and where in the long run everybody, good and evil alike, becomes known by his true name . . . That is the fairy tale of the Gospel with, of course, one crucial difference from all other fairy tales, which is that the claim made for it is that it is true, that it not only happened once upon a time, but has kept on happening ever since and is happening still (Telling the Truth).*

*This is the gospel.*

*This is the Story we are living in.*

*May you play your part well."*
— JOHN ELDREDGE

Before we move on to the final jump, let's consider the following wisdom for you to making this Epic Jump into reality.

In the movie, "The Last Samurai," the line from the Emperor to the Samurai was: "tell me how did he die" and the Samurai says to the Emperor, "I will tell you how he lived."

That is the Epic Jump. How did we live? What did we leave behind that says, as in the movie, "Gladiator," when Maximus says to his troops before they go into battle: "What we do in life echoes in eternity."

Our lives matter, no matter how small or insignificant we think they are, we are all precious, especially to the One who created all. Your life will echo in this life and the after. Not by what we gained, but by what we contributed, the jumps we took. There are units that measure the worth of a man, regardless of birth. Not, "What was his station?" But "Had he a heart?" And "How did he play his God-given part?" Was he ever ready with a word of good cheer, to bring back a smile, to banish a tear? Not, "What was his share?" "What was his creed?" But "had he befriended those really in need?" Not "what did the sketch in the newspaper say?" But "How many were sorry when he passed away?"

St. Augustine said that asking yourself the question of your own legacy, what do I wish to be remembered for? Is the beginning of adulthood.

Our Epic Jump will be unique to us, just as each life and spirit is unique as the snowflakes that fall. No one is the same.

In Michelangelo's painting on the ceiling of the Sis-tine Chapel, the finger of God approaches – but does not touch, the finger of Adam. That means we never fully achieve what we set out to do – always needing more time to add the finishing touch, always stretching, always reaching, always discovering what is pos- sible. Michelangelo, on his death bed, said "I am dying just as I am learning the alphabet of my profession."

> *"Be as a stone cast upon the water, that the positive influence of your actions may extend far beyond the power of a mere pebble in the hand of men."*
>
> —ANCIENT SAYING

We are the essential, immutable links in this Epic Life we can live. "The clock of life is wound but once" – we should not fear that life will pass too quickly and come to an end. Our concern should be that we have a beginning and a middle that we can celebrate. For it is not so much what we have left undone in our incomplete life that matters as much as what we have contributed.

Ralph Waldo Emerson said, "What lies behind us, and what lies before us, are tiny matters compared to what lies within us."

We are the only ones like us who will ever live, Herschel wrote in 1965: "I am an average man. To my heart I'm a great moment. The challenge I face is how to actualize, how to concentrize the great eminence of my being."

That's the Epic Jump we must continue to leap into.

We are not supposed to do this life alone. We are to do this Epic Jump together, with others. Yes, sometimes solo like the hero's journey, but jumping with others brings much more joy, love, happiness and beauty.

I remember in high school, an epic jump for me was trying out for the football and hockey teams in Addison Illinois. I am, and was, only 5'8 and at the time, weighed about 145 pounds. I certainly wasn't linebacker or running back material! Epic jumps don't mean you have to do a triathlon or start a company or discover a cure for cancer. They could be, but small epic, Geronimo jumps are just as significant. For example, my adolescent friend, Jim Logan, who was a very talented athlete, encouraged me to try out, and that belief in me meant a lot. No one does it alone. He persuaded me to lift weights six days a week in his basement with another friend. I soon discovered I could play football and hockey with a good amount of practice. While I might not have been the biggest, strongest, or fastest, I knew I could support the team. I realized being part of a team was more valuable that going solo. Even though solo is rewarding in ways, I learned that bringing others along was better. More support meant more energy, more gifts, and more ideas.

From this early experience, I determined my gift was just that – finding others with unique strengths and bringing people together to build small businesses, teams, retreats, even softball teams. I believe that by involving others and looking for others, as I just read this morning in a blog entitled, Horizontal Leadership, is the key to any success, critical to any epic jump. The blog described a business school student putting a note in a fellow student's mailbox that said, "I'm organizing a five-person brainstorming group, and I hoping you can join us." Think about that idea. What group could you assemble and for what purpose? This person realized that the best way forward, the best jump, would be to reach out and collaborate with others. By assembling a few others, he created magic, possibility, and connection. What can you create today? It might be the start of something epic!

This notion of doing something epic is what inspired me to write this book. I wanted to pass something on to my family – something I could leave behind to hopefully inspire them in their epic lives. That's where my joy, love, and excitement comes from. Passing wisdom to others to see them change themselves and their circle of influence.

I pass on to you two poems that have helped me in my Epic Jumps in life, that you may embrace and derive truth and courage from them. This first one is meant to help bring out your epic possibilities.

## COMMITMENT

*Until one is committed,*
*There is always hesitancy,*
*The chance to draw back,*
*Always ineffectiveness.*
*Concerning all acts*
*of initiative (and creation),*
*There is one elementary truth—*
*the ignorance of which*
*kills countless ideas*
*and splendid plans:*
*that the moment*
*one definitely commits oneself,*
*then Providence moves too.*
*All sorts of things occur*
*to help one*
*that would never*
*otherwise have occurred.*
*A whole stream of events*
*issues from the decision,*
*raising in one's favor*
*all manner of unforeseen*
*incidents and meetings,*

*and material assistance,*
*which no man*
*could have dreamed*
*would have ever come his way.*
*Whatever you can do,*
*or dream you can,*
*begin it. Boldness has genius,*
*power*
*and magic in it,*
*Begin it now.*

— JOHANN WOLFGANG VON GOETHE

This next poem will give you the wisdom and worlds to help you discern the path to your epic life. Let it guide your choices of where you go, and who you involve.

## DESIDERATA

*Go placidly amid the noise and haste,*
*and remember what peace there may be in silence.*
*As far as possible without surrender*
*be on good terms with all persons.*
*Speak your truth quietly and clearly;*
*and listen to others,*
*even the dull and the ignorant;*
*they too have their story.*

*Avoid loud and aggressive persons,*
*they are vexations to the spirit.*
*If you compare yourself with others,*
*you may become vain and bitter;*
*for always there will be greater and lesser persons than yourself.*
*Enjoy your achievements as well as your plans.*

*Keep interested in your own career, however humble;*
*it is a real possession in the changing fortunes of time.*
*Exercise caution in your business affairs;*
*for the world is full of trickery.*
*But let this not blind you to what virtue there is;*
*many persons strive for high ideals;*
*and everywhere life is full of heroism.*

*Be yourself.*
*Especially, do not feign affection.*
*Neither be cynical about love;*
*for in the face of all aridity and disenchantment*
*it is as perennial as the grass.*
*Take kindly the counsel of the years,*
*gracefully surrendering the things of youth.*
*Nurture strength of spirit to shield you in sudden misfortune.*

*But do not distress yourself with dark imaginings.*
*Many fears are born of fatigue and loneliness.*
*Beyond a wholesome discipline,*
*be gentle with yourself.*

*You are a child of the universe,*
*no less than the trees and the stars;*
*you have a right to be here.*
*And whether or not it is clear to you,*
*no doubt the universe is unfolding as it should.*

*Therefore be at peace with God, whatever you conceived Him to he,*
*and whatever your labors and aspirations,*
*in the noisy confusion of live keep peace with your soul.*

*With all its sham, drudgery, and broken dreams,*
*it is still a beautiful world.*
*Be cheerful.*

—MAX EHRMANN, DESIDERATA, COPYRIGHT 1952

# EPIC JUMP

---

## JUMPING CALLS TO ACTION

- What's one area in life you can become more curious in, go deeper with? Write it and for the next 6 weeks discover all you can.

- Practice "Wonder" instead of Worry. Wonder how this could change, how this could be different. Wonder about your possibilities in life. Wonder if you take that jump today how that could change the way you live.

- Write down your legacy. What do you want people to say about your life? How do you want to be remembered? Take an early morning and reflect on this and write it in your Epic journal. Write your name in bold letters and realize what you do in life really does echo in eternity.

- What group could you start? Which five people can you involve? What can be a common goal for you?

# GERONIMO JUMP 8

---

# EVERLASTING JUMP

*"All longings are a longing for God."*

—ST. AUGUSTINE 354–430 AD

The most difficult – or easiest – Jump in your life will be the Everlasting Jump. The Everlasting Jump is the Jump in which you know that you are part of a greater plan, a greater you, a greater cause. You realize that your life was not an accident but part of a higher purpose – that this world could not just be a happenstance but part of a divine touch by a divine creator, and that you are part of that amazing inception. Before taking this jump you will decide in your heart if you believe this to be true. You will ask yourself, am I part of this grand creation? Or you will tell yourself this is all a grand illusion. This Geronimo Jump is where you surrender all, not just some, and you believe that surrendering will set you free to truly trust that you have been given a gift that once opened can never be taken back. It is a gift that keeps on giving, a gift that reveals your true identity, essence and beauty. You belong to a kingdom that will never end and your place in this kingdom is a unique, beautiful and special mission if you choose to accept the gift.

Will you harden your heart or open your heart? Will you close your hands into a fist or will you release your fingers and reach up? Will you believe or doubt? Will you open your eyes, receive the eternal touch, breathe in life, breathe in spirit, breath in truth? Whether or not you have taken the other seven leaps, without this leap, it all will be meaningless.

There is a story of a fish that jumped onto the land. It was struggling to breathe so someone gave the fish a million dollars. The fish still was struggling. Someone gave the fish a beautiful mansion, cars, boats, all the stuff, and still the fish was losing his breath. Someone even gave the fish the title of king and royal majesty, but still the fish struggled for his life. Finally, someone threw the fish back into the water and suddenly the fish regained his breath and life. The water saved him just as God is willing to save us, whether we achieve all the other 7 leaps or accumulate a million dollars. All of that is meaningless. By this I mean, if you make all the other jumps and resist the everlasting Jump, the previous ones will not bring lasting love, meaning, or purpose. This fish in the story is you and me. We have everything but we have nothing. Go ask Solomon. Solomon was a man who asked God for wisdom. God told him he could ask for anything and he chose wisdom. He was a young man of 14 or 15, who was to be the next king in the land, and he was fearful of not making the right decisions for his people. So he asked for wisdom, and God granted it. He was noted as the wisest and richest man in history. People from all countries traveled hundreds of miles on foot or horse to seek his counsel. Solomon's wealth was inconceivable, and at one point he sought the pleasures of this world by building massive homes, had hundreds of wives, and daily parties filled with dance, music, and wine. In the end, he said it was all meaningless. "All the wealth and excess means nothing if God is not in it, and if I seek all the treasures of the world and leave God out it, a void in my soul opens that only the creator can fill." Go read his story in the Great Book of Wisdom.

Remember the movie, "The Book of Eli" with Denzel Washington. While there is some violence in the film, Denzel's character carries the last Bible across the land to find a home for it because all others have been lost, buried, or destroyed. Until we come home, to God, to our Creator, to our destiny, we will also be lost — even if it seems we have made it in the world's eyes. All longings are a longing for God — we just don't understand or realize this. Every longing our soul has is a longing to be one, united with our God, our King, our Savior, our Lord. Some might believe they long for a Jaguar convertible, which I think looks pretty cool and wouldn't mind having. But even if we obtain the Jaguar, a few days later our soul longs for something else — a new job, a new spouse or partner, a new home. Another longing to fill our longings, when our longings can only be satisfied by filling it with God.

I am not saying don't fulfill the other seven jumps. I am not say- ing don't create wealth or enjoy this life. Just like when Iron Man, played by Robert Downey, Jr., had it all, his friend said, "you have everything and nothing." You can have it all and have nothing if your soul has not breathed in and believed that you owe every breath, each day – your life --to Him who created you.

Why do some not take this leap? Someone once asked me, "Do you know what the hardest substance in the world is, Mark?" I said a diamond. He said, "No." A ruby? No. An emerald? No. I give up. What is the hardest substance in the world? He said, "your will." Your will is the hardest substance to change, to break, to give in, to surrender. "Not my will, but your Father-in-Heaven." Remember those words by Jesus. Jesus still gave up His will even though He was God and surrendered His will to die for us. Can we not surrender our will for Him who gave everything on the cross? You might be reading this thinking I am trying to persuade you to surrender your will to Jesus. I am. But I am no fool. I am a man, a human just like you, and only you can choose the Everlasting Leap and make the God Leap. Not me, not your parents, not your lover, not your pastor, priest or rabbi. You are the one to jump, and even if someone pushed you, presented you with fear, or a hellfire sermon to motivate you to jump to God, or screamed at you that without God there is no legacy, no purpose, no grace, no freedom – without your making that God-Jump, and you alone, you won't be strong enough to brave this world and fight the good fight. You won't be able to become all you were created to be. Without this jump, the other Geronimo Jumps will end in tragedy. Will you this day, if you have not yet, just say yes to the everlasting leap and surrender your heart and mind?

Someone said the longest path in life is from your mind to your heart. Our mind is what will stop us from opening our hearts to what is truth, freedom, love, peace. Even though we say we want these things, without God, it will all be in vain. It will be a life wasted by us thinking we did it all.

God is hidden within us. Are we willing to uncover God? Let Him shine in our lives. Let Him lead. Acknowledge that with Him all things are possible and, if you choose to die, you truly live. If we die to ourselves, we actually become awake. If we take the Everlasting Leap, all the other leaps will not be in vain. Instead, all other leaps will bring deeper meaning, deeper purpose. The Everlasting Leap will carry us beyond our last breath, and our spirit will never die. We will experience Eternity with God. Our longings will finally be complete. All will be beautiful. This is the last chapter of this book. Chapter 8. There is no chapter nine.

The number 8 symbol and meaning in the Bible is "New Beginnings." Don't we all long for new beginnings each day, a new purpose, new life, new love, new wisdom, new energy, vitality, peace? Without the Everlasting Leap, the number 8, instead of being a new beginning for our souls and journey, becomes a crazy 8 that we just keep circling. We keep the patterns of this world instead of the Kingdom in our hearts and minds.

The Everlasting Jump can break chains, can set the captives free, can help the blind see, and the lame walk. Without the God leap, we are captive to the world, blind to our own ambition, walking lame; chained to our addictions, wounds, and sin. Jesus breaks the chains, opens our eyes and helps us to walk again, if we are willing to make that Jump and complete the 8 – complete the new beginning that no man, no woman, no ruler on this earth, no job, no amount of money can give. St. Augustine once said, My heart is restless until it rests in Thee.

Make the God Jump and rest in knowing that the Great I Am, the Great Father in Heaven, the Great King and Warrior will send His Spirit, His Holy breath to awaken the deep within your soul and give you new life. Yes, new birth! Yes, new beginnings so we can travel the road ahead and continue to take the Jumps, but now you Jump with the Power of God. Now you Jump with His Power in your soul. Now you jump with His passion and purpose. Now your jumps will leave a mark, a legacy. With God, you can jump with grace and compassion for others; you can jump into a deeper love for yourself, others and your Creator.

If you take this leap, you will jump with His Holy Spirit and He will carry you when the jump seems too hard, when the jump seems impossible, when the world seems to be crushing you in at all sides. He will be there to jump with you and, if need be, carry you to the other side. Yes, God will carry you to the other side. God will break through against all odds in life and leap you into Greatness. He will be your parachute. He will leap with you into the Greatness of His Kingdom and your mission, and if you choose to accept it, He is always there, always willing to lead you into the supercalifragilisticexpialidocious life.

Listen to His Voice of truth. His Voice will whisper the truth in the midnight hour. His Voice will lift you high as an eagle. He will fight the good fight with you. He will help you finish the race in life. He will help you keep to faith when your faith is failing. He is the Good Shepherd. He will guide your path. Psalm 23 tells us that He will walk through the valley of the shadow of death. Fear not for His hand will protect you and goodness and mercy will follow you all the days of your life.

The Everlasting Jump is waiting. Will you take the Jump today? Renew your leap, rediscover the Everlasting Jump again and again and again. God will always draw you deeper if you choose, and He will never leave you or forsake you. What a friend we have in Jesus. Will you Jump the Everlasting Jump that will forever change your life and destiny?

*"God has made everything beautiful for its own time. He has planted eternity in the human heart."*
—ECCLESIASTES 3:11 NLT

God has given you a heart for his kingdom. This is one of the most important things you can know about yourself. Did you know this about yourself ? When was the last time you told yourself, as you were looking the mirror, "Good morning; you have a heart for the kingdom."?

*"I will lift mine eyes unto the hills, from whence cometh my help. My help cometh from the Lord, which made Heaven and Earth."*
—PSALM 121

In the last chapter, the Everlasting Jump, I will leave you with five poems that I hope you reflect on in this great life we have been given. May your Jumps be wild, courageous, bring you vitality, renewal, joy, depth, compassion, love beyond measure.

*"God does not call us to be successful — God calls us to be faithful."*
—MOTHER TERESA

*The future has many names. For the weak, it is the impossible. For the faint-hearted, it is the unknown. For the thoughtful, it is hope.*
—VICTOR HUGO

What are you waiting for? **JUMP!**

## THE JOURNEY

*One day you finally knew what you had to do,*
*and began,*
*though the voices around*
*you kept shouting their bad advice —*
*through the whole house began to tremble*
*and you felt the old tug at your ankles.*
*"Mend my life!" each voice cried. But you didn't stop.*
*You knew what you had to do,*
*though the wind pried with its stiff fingers*
*at the very foundations,*
*though their melancholy was terrible.*

*It was already late enough,*
*and a wild night.*
 *and the road full of fallen branches and stones.*

*But little by little,*
*as you left their voices behind,*
*and the stars began to burn through the sheets of clouds,*

*and there was a new voice*
*which you slowly recognized as your own,*
*that kept you company*
*as you strode deeper and deeper into the world,*

*determined to do*
*the only thing you could do —*

*determined to save*
*the only life you could save.*
—MARY OLIVER

## AND GOD SAID, "NO"

*I asked God to take away my pride,*
*And God said, "No."*
*He said it was not for Him to take away,*
*But for me to give up.*

*I asked God to make my handicapped child whole,*
*And God said, "No."*
*He said her spirit is whole.*
*Her body is only temporary.*

*I asked God to grant me patience,*
*And God said, "No."*
*He said patience is a by-product of tribulation.*
*It isn't granted, it is earned.*

*I asked God to give me happiness,*
*And God said, "No."*
*He said He gives me blessings.*
*Happiness is up to me.*

*I asked God to spare me pain,*
*And God said, "No."*
*He said, "Suffering draws you apart from*
*worldly cares and brings you closer to Me."*

*I asked God to make my spirit grow,*
*And God said, "No."*
*He said I must grow on my own.*
*But He will prune me to make it fruitful.*

*I asked God if He loved me,*
*And God said, "Yes."*

*He gave me His only Son, who died for me.*
*Because . . . I believe.*

*I asked God to help me love others*
*as much as He loves me.*
*And God said,*
*"Ah, finally you have the idea."*
—Claudia Minden Welsz

## THE THIRTEENTH DISCIPLE

*Never doubt if Jesus Lord*
*Anointed but a few,*
*His breath upon the Chosen Twelve,*
*His Life in them renewed.*

*In Him there witnessed Light Divine*
*With Tongues to speak to all,*
*Disciples of Almighty Christ,*
*Disciples of His Call.*

*But were it only just these Twelve*
*That Jesus called to life?*
*Is there perchance a Thirteenth love*
*To stand beside His Might?*

*Where you too can feel a loving Hand*
*Caress and guide your heart.*
*A trail of faith, that's all you need,*
*A light unto the dark.*

*And birds to tilt you skyward*
*For the blessings of the day,*

*Rain to bring you blossoms,*
*A sun to grace your way.*

*To bow before His dazzling Son,*
*A knee, a self, now bent.*

*Transformed by light and wind and heat*
*This child in full ascent.*

*And so come close, like Peter, James,*
*So chosen and adored.*
*You're now a living legend,*
*Thirteenth disciple of our Lord.*

— JOYCE GRAHAM

## DISTURB US, LORD

*Disturb us, Lord, when*
*We are too well pleased with ourselves,*
*When our dreams have come true*
*Because we have dreamed  too little,*
*When we arrived safely*
*Because we sailed too close to the shore.*

*Disturb us, Lord, when*
*With the abundance of things we possess*
*We have lost our thirst*
*For the waters of life;*
*Having fallen in love with life,*
*We have ceased to dream of eternity*
*And in our efforts to build a new earth,*
*We have allowed our vision*
*Of the new Heaven to dim.*

*Disturb us, Lord, to dare more boldly,*
*To venture on wider seas*
*Where storms will show your mastery;*
*Where losing sight of land,*
*We shall find the stars.*

*We as You to push back The*
*horizons of our hopes; And*
*to push into the future*
*In strength, courage, hope and love.*

—ATTRIBUTED TO SIR FRANCIS DRAKE – 1577

## THE STATION

Tucked away in our subconscious is an idyllic vision. We see ourselves on a long trip that spans the continent. We are traveling by train. Out the windows we drink in the passing scene of cars on nearby highways, of children waving at a crossing, of cattle grazing on a distant hillside, of smoke pouring from a power plant, of row upon row of corn and wheat, of flatlands and valleys, of mountains and rolling hillsides, of city skylines and village halls.

But uppermost in our minds is the final destination. Bands will be playing and flags waving. Once we get there our dreams will come true, and the pieces of our lives will fit together like a jigsaw puzzle.

How restlessly we pace the aisles, damning the minutes for loitering, waiting, waiting, waiting for the station.

"When we reach the station, that will be it!" we cry.

"When I'm 18."

"When I buy a new 450SL Mercedes-Benz!"

"When I put the last kid through college."

"When I have paid off the mortgage!"

"When I get a promotion."

"When I reach the age of retirement, I shall live happily ever after!"

*Sooner or later we must realize there is no station, no one place to arrive at once and for all. The true joy of life is the trip. The station is only a dream. It constantly outdistances us.*

*"Relish the moment" is a good motto, especially when coupled with Psalm 118:24: "This is the day which the Lord hath made: we will rejoice and be glad in it." It isn't the burdens of today that drive men mad. It is the regrets over yesterday and the fear of tomorrow.*

*Regret and fear are twin thieves who rob us of today. So stop pacing the aisles and counting the miles. Instead, climb more mountains, eat more ice cream, go barefoot more often, swim more rivers, watch more sunsets, laugh more, cry less. Life must be lived as we go along. That station will come soon enough."*

—Robert J. Hastings

## PRAYER BY A CONFEDERATE SOLDIER

Sometimes, when I pray, I think all I get are busy signals or wrong numbers. But God is working in ways that, if I'll just hang in there, I'll see His hand—as evidenced in this familiar prayer by a Confederate solider:

*I asked God for strength, that I might achieve,*
*I was made weak, that I might learn humbly to obey.*
*I asked for health, that I might do greater things,*
*I was given infirmity that I might do better things.*
*I asked for riches, that I might be happy*
*I was given poverty that I might be wise.*
*I asked for power that I might have the praise of men,*
*I was given weakness, that I might feel the need of God.*

*I asked for all things, that I might enjoy life,*
*I was given life, that I might enjoy all things.*
*I got nothing that I asked for*

*But everything I had hoped for.*
*Almost despite myself,*
*My unspoken prayers were answered.*
*I am among all men, most richly blessed.*

That's the way of the Lord. In the middle of our own civil wars, we may not see God's hand. But on the other side, we'll say, "Lord, I got nothing I asked for — but everything I really wanted." The purpose and the power of prayer are not to get your way for your life, but to get the Lord's blessing on your life.

# EVERLASTING JUMP

## JUMPING CALLS TO ACTION

- Ask yourself, where would I go if my life ended today? What do I believe? Is there something beyond my vision I can't see or imagine?

- Remember, each day God says, "Show up." How can I show up daily whether for my work, my health, my family or my signifi- cant others? How can I show up better in life? List 5 areas in which you can show up more deeply.

- Ask God to reveal Himself to you through His Word, through nature, through His Son, through a trial. Ask for a miracle in life. Know God is bigger and with Him all jumps are possible!

# SUGGESTED READING LIST

The following books are listed in no particular order. All of them are designed to help in all areas of life. Develop your personal library of books to grow, develop and lead a supercalifragilisticexpialidocious life. Jim Rohn says "miss a meal if you have to, but don't miss a book." Start by reading at least one book a month. This alone will change your life, your ability to build wealth, your relationships, and your potential for greatness. "JUMP"

*Wild at Heart* . . . . . . . . . . . . . . . . . . . . . . . . . . . . . . . . . . . . . . . . . . . . . . . . . . . . John Eldredge

*The Greatest Coach Ever* . . . . . . . . . . . . . . . . . . . . . . . . . . . . . . . . . . . . . . John Wooden

*The On Purpose Person* . . . . . . . . . . . . . . . . . . . . . . . . . . . . . . . . . . . . . . Kevin McCarthy

*The Wild Man's Journey* . . . . . . . . . . . . . . . . . . . . . . . . . . . . . . . . . . . . . .Richard Rohr

*The Purpose Driven Life* . . . . . . . . . . . . . . . . . . . . . . . . . . . . . . . . . . . . . . . Rich Warren

*The War of Art* . . . . . . . . . . . . . . . . . . . . . . . . . . . . . . . . . . . . . . . . . . . . Steven Pressfield

*Legacy: The Giving of Life's Greatest Treasurers* . . . . . . . . . . . . . .Barrie Sanford Greiff

*The Way of the Small* . . . . . . . . . . . . . . . . . . . . . . . . . . . . . . . . . . . . . . . . . .Michael Gellert

*The Spiritual Teaching of Marcus Aurelius* . . . . . . . . . . . . . . . . . . . . . . . Mark Forstater

*Love Does* . . . . . . . . . . . . . . . . . . . . . . . . . . . . . . . . . . . . . . . . . . . . . . . . . . . . . . . Bob Goff

*A Better Way to Live* . . . . . . . . . . . . . . . . . . . . . . . . . . . . . . . . . . . . . . . . .Og Mandino

*Richest Man in Babylon* . . . . . . . . . . . . . . . . . . . . . . . . . . . . . . . . . . . George S. Clason

*The Success Playbook for Everyone* . . . . . . . . . . . . . . . . . . . . . . . . . .Andrew Guinosso

*Eat Your Peas For Someone Special* . . . . . . . . . . . . . . . . . . . . . . . . . . . . Cheryl Karpen

*The Gifts of Imperfection* . . . . . . . . . . . . . . . . . . . . . . . . . . . . . . . . . . . . .Brene Brown

*The Prophet* . . . . . . . . . . . . . . . . . . . . . . . . . . . . . . . . . . . . . . . . . . . . . . . . .Kahlil Gibran

*Contentment: The Secret to a Lasting Calm* . . . . . . . . . . . . . . . . . . . . .Richard Swenson

*Epic: The Story God is Telling* . . . . . . . . . . . . . . . . . . . . . . . . . . . . . . . . .John Eldredge

*Seven Strategies of Wealth and Happiness* . . . . . . . . . . . . . . . . . . . . . . . . . . .Jim Rohn

*Falling Upward* . . . . . . . . . . . . . . . . . . . . . . . . . . . . . . . . . . . . . . . . . . . . . .Richard Rohr

*The Four Agreements* . . . . . . . . . . . . . . . . . . . . . . . . . . . . . . . . . . . . . . Don Miguel Ruiz

*Captivating: Unveiling the Mystery of a Woman's Soul* . . . . . . . John & Stasi Eldredge

*So Long Insecurity* . . . . . . . . . . . . . . . . . . . . . . . . . . . . . . . . . . . . . . . . . . .Beth Moore

*The Shack* . . . . . . . . . . . . . . . . . . . . . . . . . . . . . . . . . . . . . . . . . . . . . . William P. Young

*The Silence of Adam* . . . . . . . . . . . . . . . . . . . . . . . . . . . . . . . . . . . . . . . . . . . .Larry Crabb

*Mystery of God's Will* . . . . . . . . . . . . . . . . . . . . . . . . . . . . . . . . . . . . .Charles R. Swindoll

*Start with Why* . . . . . . . . . . . . . . . . . . . . . . . . . . . . . . . . . . . . . . . . . . . . . . . Simon Sinek

*Good to Great* . . . . . . . . . . . . . . . . . . . . . . . . . . . . . . . . . . . . . . . . . . . . . . . . .Jim Collins

*Leadership 101: What Every Leader Needs to Know* . . . . . . . . . . . . . John C. Maxwell

*Even Eagles Need a Push* . . . . . . . . . . . . . . . . . . . . . . . . . . . . . . . . . . . . David McNally

*Man's Search for Meaning* . . . . . . . . . . . . . . . . . . . . . . . . . . . . . . . . . . . Viktor E. Frankl

*The Prayer of Jabez* . . . . . . . . . . . . . . . . . . . . . . . . . . . . . . . . . . . . . . .Bruce Wilkinson

*As a Man Thinketh* . . . . . . . . . . . . . . . . . . . . . . . . . . . . . . . . . . . . . . . . . James Allen

*The Road Less Traveled* . . . . . . . . . . . . . . . . . . . . . . . . . . . . . . . . . . . . M. Scott Peck

*7 Habits of Highly Effective People* . . . . . . . . . . . . . . . . . . . . . . . . . . . Stephen R. Covey

*Mastery: The Keys to Success and Long Term Fulfillment* . . . . . . . . . George Leonard

*There's a Spiritual Solution to Every Problem* . . . . . . . . . . . . . . . . . . . . Wayne W. Dyer

*Psycho Cybernetics* . . . . . . . . . . . . . . . . . . . . . . . . . . . . . . . . . . . . . . . . . .Maxwell Maltz

*Five Major Pieces to Life's Puzzle* . . . . . . . . . . . . . . . . . . . . . . . . . . . . . . . . . . Jim Rohn

*Like a Virgin: Secrets They Won't Tell You in Business School* . . . . . . Richard Branson

*Second Innocence: Rediscovering Joy and Wonder* . . . . . . . . . . . . . . . .John B. Izzo

*Uncommon Life* . . . . . . . . . . . . . . . . . . . . . . . . . . . . . . . . . . . . . . . . . . . Tony Dungy

*Seasons of Life* . . . . . . . . . . . . . . . . . . . . . . . . . . . . . . . . . . . . . . . . . . . . Jeffrey Marx

*The Ultimate Journey* . . . . . . . . . . . . . . . . . . . . . . . . . . . . . . . . . . . . . . . .Jim Stovall

*Game Plan: Winning Strategies for the Second Half of Your Life* . . . . . . . . Bob Buford

*Keep Going: The Art of Perseverance* . . . . . . . . . . . . . . . . . . . . . . . . . Joseph Marshall

*The Ideal Team Player* . . . . . . . . . . . . . . . . . . . . . . . . . . . . . . . . . . . Patrick M. Lencioni

*Boundaries for Leaders* . . . . . . . . . . . . . . . . . . . . . . . . . . . . . . . . . . . . .Henry Cloud

*Lynchpin* . . . . . . . . . . . . . . . . . . . . . . . . . . . . . . . . . . . . . . . . . . . . . . . . . Seth Godin

*Cherish: The One Word That Changes Everything for Your Marriage* .Gary Thomas

*What's So Amazing About Grace* . . . . . . . . . . . . . . . . . . . . . . . . . . . . . . .Philip Yancey

*Lead with Humility: 12 Leadership Lessons from Pope Francis* . . . . . . . Jeffrey Krames

*If You Want to Walk on Water, You've Got to Get Out of the Boat* . . . . . .John Ortberg

*Seven Principles for Making Marriage Work* . . . . . . . . . John Gottman and Nan Silver

*Kingdom Man: Every Man's Destiny, Every Woman's Dream* . . . . . . . . . . . Tony Evans

*It is Finished: 7 Stops in the Quest for Rest* . . . . . . . . . . . . . . . . . . . Peter-John Courson

*When God Winks* . . . . . . . . . . . . . . . . . . . . . . . . . . . . . . . . . . . . . . . . Squire Rushnell

*Chicken Soup for the Entrepreneur's Soul* . . . . . . . . . . . . . . . . . . . . . . . . . . . Tom Hill

*Release Your Brilliance* . . . . . . . . . . . . . . . . . . . . . . . . . . . . . . . . . . . . .Simon T. Bailey

*The Compound Effect* . . . . . . . . . . . . . . . . . . . . . . . . . . . . . . . . . . . . . . Darren Hardy

*Next Generation Leader* . . . . . . . . . . . . . . . . . . . . . . . . . . . . . . . . . . . . . Andy Stanley

*Relationship Magic: Waking Up Together* . . . . . . . . . . . . . . . . . . . . . . . . Guy Finley

*My Utmost for His Highest Devotional* . . . . . . . . . . . . . . . . . . . . . . . Oswald Chambers

*The One Minute Manager* . . . . . . . . . . . . . . . . . . . . . . . . . . . . . . . . . . . . . . Ken Blanchard

*Raving Fans* . . . . . . . . . . . . . . . . . . . . . . . . . . . . . . . . . . . . . . . . . . . . . . Ken Blanchard

*Questions Are The Answers* . . . . . . . . . . . . . . . . . . . . . . . . . . . . . . . . . . . Mel Brodsky

*Streams in the Desert Devotional* . . . . . . . . . . . . . . . L.B.E. Cowman and Jim Reimann

*Jon Courson's Application Commentaries* . . . . . . . . . . . . . . . . . . . . . . . Jon Courson

*A Mustard Seed: A Daily Devotional* . . . . . . . . . . . . . . . . . . . . . . . . . . Angus Buchan

*On The Threshold Of Transformation* . . . . . . . . . . . . . . . . . . . . . . . . . . Richard Rohr

*Mere Christianity* . . . . . . . . . . . . . . . . . . . . . . . . . . . . . . . . . . . . . . . . . . C.S. Lewis

*The Screwtape Letters* . . . . . . . . . . . . . . . . . . . . . . . . . . . . . . . . . . . . . . . C.S. Lewis

*Jonathan Livingston Seagull* . . . . . . . . . . . . . . . . . . . . . . . . . . . . . . . . . Richard Bach

*Walking In Wonder* . . . . . . . . . . . . . . . . . . . . . . . . . . . . . . . . . . . . . John O'Donahue

# AUDIO/PODCASTS/DVD'S
## TO JUMP START YOUR LIFE

Jon Courson's Teachings . . . . . . . . . . . . . . . . . . . . . . . . . . . . . Applegatefellowship.org

Jim Rohn's teachings . . . . . . . . . . . . . . . . . . . . . . . . . . . . . . . . . . . . . . . JimRohn.com

Guy Finley's teachings . . . . . . . . . . . . . . . . . . . . . . . . . . . . . . . . . . . . . guyfinley.org

Richard Rohr's teachings . . . . . . . . . . . . . . . . . . . . . . . . . . . . . . . . . . . . . . . cac.org

John Eldredge teachings . . . . . . . . . . . . . . . . . . . . . . . . . . . . . . ransomedheart.com

John Maxwell's teachings . . . . . . . . . . . . . . . . . . . . . . . . . . . . . . johnmaxwell.com

Simon T. Bailey's teachings . . . . . . . . . . . . . . . . . . . . . . . . . . . . . simontbailey.com

Patrick Lencioni's teachings . . . . . . . . . . . . . . . . . . . . . . . . . . . . . . . . tablegroup.com

Seth Godin teachings . . . . . . . . . . . . . . . . . . . . . . . . . . . . . . . . . . . . sethgodin.com

Darren Hardy's teachings . . . . . . . . . . . . . . . . . . . . . . . . . . . . dd.darrenhardy.com

Tom Hill's teachings . . . . . . . . . . . . . . . . . . . . . . . . . . . . . . . . . . . . . . drtomhill.com

Dave Ramsey's teachings . . . . . . . . . . . . . . . . . . . . . . . . . . . . . . . Daveramsey.com

# FINAL DEDICATIONS

*When a man truly loves a woman, she becomes his weakness. When a woman truly loves a man, he becomes her strength. This is called the exchange of power.*

*Thank you, Christine Mary Battiato, for all your strength and dedication to my life and our children. Without you, this would not have been written and my life would have been incomplete and many jumps would never have happened.*

*I hope you will forever jump into my arms and you will jump into all that God has created you to be.*

*I love you.*

—MARK

As I mentioned, good things come in threes. The last two beautiful women that I want to give thanks to are my Mother, Donna Battiato, who is a woman of consistency, dedication, humility and unconditional love. Thank you, Mom for giving me life and support in all things. Lastly, Deb Castillo, my business partner for over 20 years. A true mentor, guide, and friend who is not just dedicated to her vocation but her family, her spouse, her friends, her life-long learning. Thank you for all you do for our work, vocation and family.

*P.S. Brandon and Sophia: Thank you for bringing your Dad a whole new life from the beginning when you were both born. Your jumping into the world, and jumping into my life has given me the strength, determination and grit to fight the good fight, to keep the faith and finish strong. My hope for you both in your lives is that you will continue to take the Geronimo Jumps, create a dozen or more new ones and speak and write about how to live the supercalifragilisticexpialidocious life. You both were created by God to embrace, empower and impact this beautiful life and oth- ers. You are blessed on this magnificent journey.*

*Geronimo! I love you both for your amazing lives and gifts! To Dream the Impos- sible Dream. Keep jumping!*

—LOVE, DAD

## The Impossible Dream

*To dream the impossible dream*
*To fight the unbeatable foe*
*To bear with unbearable sorrow*
*To run where the brave dare not go*
*To right the unrightable wrong*
*To love pure and chaste from afar*
*To try when your arms are too weary*
*To reach the unreachable star*
*This is my quest*
*To follow that star*
*No matter how hopeless*
*No matter how far*
*To fight for the right*
*Without question or pause*
*To be willing to march into Hell*
*For a heavenly cause*
*And I know if I'll only be true*
*To this glorious quest*
*That my heart will lie peaceful and calm*
*When I'm laid to my rest*
*And the world will be better for this*
*That one man, scorned and covered with scars*
*Still strove with his last ounce of courage*
*To reach the unreachable star*

—LYRICS BY JOE DARION FROM 1965 BROADWAY MUSICAL 'MAN OF LA MANCHA"

*For a special singing version of this song, Impossible Dream, youtube, "Impossible Dream" Luther Vandross, Live.*

# AUTHOR'S NOTE

Thank you for taking the time to jump with me through these eight chapters. My hope for this world, this new generation, for young teenagers, for married couples, for people who are retired, grandparents, young entrepreneurs, people who have jumped and failed, have been put down, abused, been in AA, felt all alone – is that this small book will give you hope.

One time I received a phone call from a friend who had been devastated by something very personal and dear in his life, and was near the brink of just throwing it all away. He told me this life was not worth living. What do you say to someone who says that? And knowing that we all have been ready to say that at one time or another, I could relate to my friend.

I was silent for a moment. Then, I don't know how, but I said, "Do you know what the word Hope stands for?" He said no. I didn't know what I was going to say next, but then, as Bill Bailey says, "the words came out." I don't question the source. I then said, Hope stands for: Heaven Opens Possibilities Every day. My friend was silent for a few moments, then he finally thanked me for those words. I had never forgotten them.

I didn't say "Jump," then. He might have gone to the San Francisco Bridge and did just that, because he lived close to it. Hope is a beautiful thing, my friends. Heaven does open possibilities every day! Listen, look, believe, jump, for God is with us in everyone.

—MARK

# ABOUT THE AUTHOR

**MARK BATTIATO**

In over three decades of business and life coaching, Mark Battiato, co-founder of the Growth into Greatness Institute, shares the eight Geronimo jumps to create a supercalifragilisticexpialidocious life. We must all continue to jump in life to become all we are capable of becoming. Where do I start? What jumps are most vital? Why should I make these jumps? What impact in life can I possibly have?

The eight Geronimo jumps in this book will give you a blueprint and game plan for discovering how to create the incredible life you are meant to live. We all need guides, mentors, or people who walked before us. In these pages, there is much wisdom from men and women from the past and now who can guide us to greatness, who can help us proclaim, "Geronimo!" and make our jumps in life echo in to eternity!

# GERONIMO

## 8 JUMPS TO A
## SUPERCALIFRAGILISTICEXPIALODOCIOUS LIFE

To contact Mark Battiato email him at
**mark@greatnessinstitute.com**
or go to
**greatnessinstitute.com**
and click on Geronimo link to go to additional resources, tools,
CDs from William E. Bailey, speaking engagements: keynote,
full or half day seminars on the 8 Geronimo jumps.

Made in the USA
Middletown, DE
24 January 2020